ENTERING THE HOUSEHOLD OF GOD

ENTERING THE HOUSEHOLD OF GOD

TAKING BAPTISM SERIOUSLY IN A POST-CHRISTIAN SOCIETY

CLAUDIA A. DICKSON

 CHURCH

Church Publishing Incorporated, New York

Library of Congress Cataloging-in-Publication Data

Dickson, Claudia A.
Entering the household of God: taking baptism seriously in a post-christian society/
    by Claudia A. Dickson.
p. cm.
    ISBN 0898693640 (pbk.)
    1. Baptism—Episcopal Church. 2. Episcopal Church—Doctrines—I. Title.
    BX5949.B2 .D53 20002
    264'.36—dc21   2002023399

Church Publishing Incorporated
445 Fifth Avenue
New York NY 10016

www.churchpublishing.org

5 4 3 2 1

For Gil, whose love, encouragement and insights made it possible for me to write this book and for our children, Caleb and Emily.

CONTENTS

ACKNOWLEDGMENTS

In the fall of 1986 while pursuing a Master of Divinity degree at Yale Divinity School I took a course on Baptism taught by Father Aidan Kavanagh that inspired me to think about this sacrament in a new light. While serving at Christ Church Cathedral in Hartford, Connecticut, I formed a Lay Catechists Group whose members met with me on a regular basis between 1992 and 1994 to discuss the theology of baptism and develop a program for preparing candidates for receiving this sacrament. I am most thankful for their participation and commitment. The Rev. Ken Henry and the Vestry of St. Michael's Episcopal Church, Raleigh, North Carolina, graciously granted me a sabbatical in the fall of 1999, which provided me with the time to organize my thoughts and write this book. Paul Elliott read the manuscript early on and his enthusiastic observations were most encouraging. I am grateful to Frank Tedeschi of Church Publishing, Inc. for accepting my book for publication, with special thanks due to Joan Castagnone who edited it with great care and insight. Furthermore, these acknowledgments would not be complete without mentioning the members of St. Michael's Episcopal Church among whom I have ministered for the past seven and a half years. A priest could not ask for a more supportive and engaging parish family. And lastly, I am indebted to my husband, the Rev. Dr. Gil Greggs, who faithfully lives out his baptismal vows daily and whose many suggestions and ideas are found in the pages of this book.

Easter 2002
Raleigh, North Carolina

RECLAIMING BAPTISMAL FAITH

*We receive you into the household of God. Confess
the faith of Christ crucified, proclaim his resurrection,
and share with us in his eternal priesthood.**

About fourteen years ago, in the first parish I served after
seminary, a woman called the church inquiring about having
her daughter baptized. She was listed on the church's rolls, but as
far as anyone could tell hadn't actually been to church in years. I
was looking forward to getting to know her as I drove to her house.

However, early in our conversation she told me quite frankly
she had no intention of coming back to church. I was totally
confused. I couldn't understand why—if she didn't want to be a
part of our church community, or of any church for that matter—
having her daughter baptized was so important to her. After all,
baptism is about belonging to a Christian community. Why
would anyone want to join something in which they have no
intention of participating? "Well," she explained, "it's what my
family has always done. When you have a baby, you're just supposed
to go on and get her baptized."

---

* The Service of Holy Baptism, The Book of Common Prayer (New York: Church
Hymnal Corporation, 1979) 308. Hereafter referred to as BCP.

For many people today, people who would define themselves as Christian, baptism is no longer the step a person takes—on their own behalf or on behalf of their child—when they are ready to give their allegiance to Jesus Christ. No longer does it imply for them that they will devote their lives to serving God and God's people within the context of membership in a Christian community. Indeed, for many people baptism has become simply a reflex action. Something you automatically have done when your baby is born, a cultural rite of passage, rather than an initiation into a way of life and a community of faith.

Certainly for Jesus, baptism was not a reflex action. Nor could it have been for Peter when he baptized new converts to Christianity. And certainly, it was not the case in the early church when, in order to be baptized, people spent up to three years studying and performing works of charity. Back then, being baptized was a radical break from the norms of society that could have gotten you killed.

Indeed, baptism started out as something countercultural. It may be hard to think of it that way now. Babies in lacey white gowns do not appear in the least to be revolutionaries. Yet, baptism should be seen as a radical step in anyone's life. In the early church people spent three years in preparation because it took time to begin to unlearn habits and assumptions that everyone took for granted, but ran counter to Christianity.

New Christians had to learn to stop judging people by how much money they made, to stop assuming that poor people deserved their fate, to stop indulging desires regardless of the consequences—all things society took for granted. People who wanted to live life as Christians had to learn to discipline their thoughts and actions, to desire virtue rather than to gratify vice, to take up works of charity, and to begin to place the needs of others ahead of their own. In short, they had to learn to live like disciples, because to be baptized is to become a disciple.

And while the twenty-first century certainly looks much different than the first, the tensions between our cultural norms and Christian faith are just as strong. Turn on the television today and we immediately receive the message that life is a competitive sport and the only way to win is to have the latest in home furnishings, clothes, and automobiles. We hear that what we do with our money is no one's darn business (including God's) and that fame is the ultimate prize and notoriety is the key to it. And finally, our natural tendency to think first of our own needs is reinforced.

Baptism is still about undertaking a countercultural way of life. It is still about learning to live like a disciple. Those of us baptized long before we had any kind of understanding of what others were promising on our behalf now need to come to terms with the implications of this sacrament on our daily life.

Are we seeking to find out what it means to be a disciple and follow Jesus? Do we ask God throughout our day to show us his will for us? Do we ask what God wants us to do with our abilities? How God wants us to conduct ourselves at work? What God wants us to pursue in life?

Do we see our financial resources as a gift from God to be used for *God's* purposes rather than our own comfort? Are we working in any way to bring about reconciliation in our world, reconciliation between those caught up in a materialistic society and those cast aside? Between those done an injustice and those who are unjust. Between those who have no hope and those who have found it in Jesus Christ?

Moreover, have we actively sought to become more virtuous? Have we taken up certain disciplines such as intercessory prayer, fasting, or daily confession in order to better discern God's direction and make us more aware of the needs of others? And are we performing acts of charity and kindness and generosity, without seeking attention or reward?

Being baptized is not about being good or polite or even a decent citizen. It's about learning to be a faithful disciple. It requires a kind of sacrifice and obedience to God that mere goodness and decency and proper manners never ask of us. Furthermore, being baptized is also about making a commitment to a community of faith. It's about joining up, about membership in the household of God.

Baptism takes place before the entire congregation, because the entire congregation is encouraged to be on hand to welcome new brothers and sisters in Christ into the fold. Newly baptized persons acquire a new kind of family, one they should expect to support them and encourage them in their new life of faith. And, in turn, newly baptized persons should expect to serve the congregation in the same way.

Thus there is no such person as a "non-active" member. To be baptized is to participate, in ways large or small, in the life of the church, regardless of whether one thinks one is getting something out of it. It's not about what you get back, but about what you give. Furthermore, there never comes a time when one can just sit back and let others serve. A life of service to God, to our church, to God's entire community is inherent in one's baptism.

Baptism is not something to be taken lightly or for granted. It is not something one does just because one's family has always done it. It is to be entered into soberly, honestly, and wholeheartedly. It is not a reflex action; it is a revolutionary way of life. Therefore, the church has an opportunity and obligation to welcome warmly and minister graciously to people who may have only a casual understanding of baptism, and help them discover the profound implications of this sacrament.

This book is for people who are preparing to have their children baptized and for people baptized long ago who wish to learn anew what having baptismal faith is all about. Lay people and clergy can use it—individually or in small groups. Section I provides background material on the evolution of baptism from its beginning to the present. Section II is designed to help structure small group discussion.

All Christians need to be in an ongoing process of "formation" where we are reminded, challenged, and encouraged to follow after Jesus Christ, and to live up to our baptismal vows, to be a disciple. This book can be a tool in such a process. My hope is that in reclaiming the radical implications of baptism we can all become more faithful members of God's church, better equipped to carry out God's work in the world.

SECTION
I

SECTION 1

CHAPTER 1

BAPTISM IS ABOUT BELONGING

"I can worship God on the golf course; I don't need to go to church in order to do that." What pastor has not heard this before, from someone who insists that he or she is just not the "church-going kind"? Yet, this person would also be likely to claim to be a good Christian. Being involved in the worship and life of a congregation is not universally viewed to be an integral part of faith by people who refer to themselves as Christian. Many people maintain that it is possible to be a Christian without belonging to a church. For them their belief in Jesus Christ is simply a matter between themselves and God.

FAITH AS A PRIVATE MATTER

There are several reasons for the prevalence of this view, particularly in the United States. First, there is the tendency to separate belief from fellowship and charitable acts. As a result, one may hold that believing in Jesus is an intellectual activity, that knowledge equals salvation, and that the Christian life entails merely affirming that Jesus is God's Son and has atoned for our sins. This kind of belief asks only that we agree to a theological statement. Some people may add that one should seek to be a good person (More about that in Chapter 3), and, perhaps, read the Bible. But these things can be done without any sort of interaction with—or commitment to—other human beings.

On television there are a number of evangelists who, perhaps inadvertently, present Christianity in this light. One can become a "believer" and worship God from the comfort of one's armchair. And of course a contribution to the evangelist's ministry is also encouraged. But to date I have heard only one evangelist on television consistently exhort his viewers to turn in faith to Jesus *and* go out and join a church.

So belief is often viewed as a private matter that involves only intellectual assent. When coupled with the tendency of Americans to pride themselves on their individualism, we have a unique form of religious expression, one in stark contrast to the one we find in the early Christian church. In these days, religious belief tends to be anti-community.

In the book, *Habits of the Heart,* the authors convincingly argue that from its inception this country has valued the kind of person who can leave the safety of community and strike out on his or her own.* Depending upon a network of fellow citizens can, in a certain light, be viewed as a sign of weakness. We have been encouraged as a nation to prize self-sufficiency. We admire our national icons—the homesteader, the cowboy of the "wild" West, the self-made millionaire—in part because it appears as though they became successful on their own, without help from anyone.

This way of thinking has inevitably affected our religious life. The same "go it alone" attitude is prevalent among many Americans who call themselves, "Christian." Historically, our culture does not encourage the notion that dependence upon one another is a good thing, particularly dependence upon people we may not

---

* Bellah, Madsen, et al., *Habits of the Heart* (Berkeley: University of California Press, 1985). See in particular Chapter 5.

even know or like. Most people would argue that they have a circle of family or friends upon whom they see themselves as reliant. However, by and large, we are not comfortable committing ourselves to a group of people whom are not relatives or friends we have chosen.

The Rise of Individualism

The roots of such autonomy, if it can be called that, go far back, to a time before the Reformation in the sixteenth century, when political and spiritual institutions ruled with complete authority. The notion of the "self" as an individual was not yet an accepted concept. In that age one's identity was derived, not as a result of differentiating oneself from others, but from belonging to a larger entity such as the family or the village. We still see this philosophy in countries of the Far East, where one values membership in a community more highly than one's identity as an individual.

This was also true in pre-Reformation Europe. Large, extended families lived close together. A man would follow the same occupation as his forebears. Everyone shared a common story or history, and it shaped who a person was, giving an identity that had been passed down from generation to generation within a particular village. Certainly no one would think of leaving behind home and family in search of one's "true" self. The community took precedence over the individual.

The authorities that ruled over this communal life were the leaders of the Catholic Church—the pope and his clergy—and the monarch. It was universally thought that the king led with divine right. His subjects gave him complete allegiance. The church played a central role in life, interpreting the meaning of faith and existence and instructing believers in how to view the world and live within it faithfully. Thinking for oneself was not yet a valued concept. One trusted these two authority systems to do that, and they worked, for the most part, hand in hand.

Yet, by the fifteenth and sixteenth centuries, the institutional authority of the church in Western Europe began to erode under the challenge of internal reforms, openly disobedient clergy and lay people, and political and cultural change. The church's formerly unchallenged dogmatic interpretation of the Bible received serious challenge, both in England and on the continent, when church reformers shocked ecclesiastical authorities by issuing unauthorized translations of the Bible.

Once it was translated from Latin into English, German, and French, people were free to read and interpret the Scriptures independently. This remarkable freedom unleashed the Bible from dogmatic constraint. Luther used his reading of the Bible very effectively to challenge the church's biblical warrant for the sale of indulgences. Scripture, he showed, advocated no such practice. We are set free from our sins, he argued, by the grace of Jesus Christ and not by the purchase of indulgences.

The church's formerly unassailable assertions about the natural world and humanity's place in it were similarly shaken by the revolutionary work of Copernicus, Galileo, and Brahe. In the face of severe persecution and harassment, each held to empirical evidence over and against church teaching that the earth was not the center of God's universe, but rather a planet in the heavens that revolved around a solar center. This was a staggering counter-claim to church teaching.

The Reformation, which was underway by the sixteenth century, greatly diminished the Catholic Church's authority. On the political front, the establishment of constitutional law in England, and, later in the eighteenth century, revolutions in America and France, led to the establishment of civil rights and individual freedoms. People were free to form new communities that were not ruled or directed by the Catholic Church and the king.

The beginning of a new age of democratic ideals—and an emphasis upon individuality—was dawning. This period, beginning in the eighteenth century, is referred to as the Enlightenment.

Determining one's own direction in life was a new and exciting possibility. The old forces that had dictated what one did in life, how one should think about oneself, and what one should believe were in decline.

These new ideals of self-determination and autonomy began to be reflected within Christian circles. It was up to the individual to choose what to believe; one did not need religious authorities for that. Each individual could be an authority unto him or herself. Communities for fellowship and worship were now being formed on the basis of common viewpoints. Commitments were conditional. Participation was voluntary.

During roughly this same period of time—between the Reformation of the sixteenth century and the Enlightenment of the eighteenth century—another movement arose that contributed to the modern notions of autonomy and privacy within Christianity. Following on the heels of Luther's reform activities, the Pietistic movement began in Germany in the 1600s. A group of German Christians, known as the Moravians, began to emphasize the importance of cultivating a personal form of piety in addition to participating in corporate worship. Developing both a personal prayer life and relationship with God was stressed. The Moravians lived a simple life, not concerned with accumulating worldly wealth. They had a great influence upon John Wesley, who founded the Methodist "reform" movement within the Anglican Church.

The Great Awakening—two waves of revivals, first in the 1700s and again in the 1800s, both in New England—followed as a result of the influences of the Pietistic movement. Jonathan Edwards, the leader of the first of the Great Awakening revivals was influenced both by democratic notions from the Enlightenment and the idea of personal salvation. This synthesis paved the way for the belief that individual action is the center of everything that is so common in religious expression today.

The sense of community wanes when the need to develop personal habits of piety outweighs the sense of oneself as part of a larger worshiping entity. The unfortunate result is that people now tend to belong to a Christian community only to the extent that it meets individual needs. What is good for the community is no longer of primary concern; what matters is what is good for the individual.

And in fact, "belonging" is no longer regarded as necessary in order to live a faithful life. One can do that on one's own. The tendency toward intellectualizing faith, combined with the desire for autonomy, accounts for the prevalence of individualistic expressions of worship in American Christianity. Many people believe that they may just as appropriately worship God on the golf course, the mountaintop, or in the privacy of their own homes as they would in a church. After all, a church is just a building. God is everywhere.

Yet many of those same people were baptized in a church. And they would be surprised to learn that an important aspect of baptism is initiation into the church—not a building, per se— but a community of faith, which represents the worldwide fellowship of Christians. The term "church" should not lead one to think of an institution or a building, but of a society of human beings who hold a common faith in Jesus Christ. Those who lived in New Testament times understood that, among other things, Christian baptism initiated a person into such a community, which was referred to as the Body of Christ. And lifelong commitment to that community was naturally assumed.

To better understand why baptism is regarded as one's initiation into a lifelong relationship with fellow members of the Body of Christ, we need to appreciate the essential role of the Holy Spirit.

COMMUNITY AS A REFLECTION OF GOD'S NATURE

Throughout the Bible we see how God's Spirit seeks to draw people together in fellowship and equips them with the attributes necessary for their communities to function well. In the second verse of the very first chapter in the Book of Genesis we are told that the Spirit of God moved over the face of the waters. As creation unfolds we are given a glimpse of how the Holy Spirit helps bring order out of chaos, community out of nothing. For indeed, God is in the business of creating communities: plants, fish, fowl, animals, and finally humans. God does not desire that anyone be on its own without the benefit of society, as evidenced in the story of Adam and Eve's creation.

In truth, God's fundamental nature is communal: Father, Son, and Holy Spirit. Each one attending to the other. Even God, though described as "one" in theological terms, is not solitary. God is simultaneously both one and triune. The three persons of the Godhead need one another and are in complete accord with one another. The Trinity is community at its perfection. In creation God seeks to have this ideal reflected in the newly formed world. And it is the Holy Spirit, the third person in the Trinity, who breathes life into a vast number of societies as creation unfolds.

Not only does the Bible describe the work of the Spirit of God as that of creating community, we see also how the Holy Spirit works to promote accord within those communities. When Moses complained to God of the burden of looking after the many needs of the Israelites in the desert (Num 11:1–30), God sent forth the Spirit to equip seventy others to assist Moses in his duties, thereby helping to maintain order in the camp.

God's Spirit also empowers persons within a community to serve in specific ways to help to maintain its health and vitality. Teachers, prophets, and leaders are all anointed by the Spirit to serve God's people and hold them together in faith. Sadly, the people of God fell into chaos and invading armies dispersed the remnants of the once mighty community of Israel that God had called together in the wilderness. However, God's Spirit showed the prophet Ezekiel how God would call forth a faithful community again (Ezek 37). We are to conclude that authentic life within a community can only be made possible through the power of the Spirit.

The Spirit's work continues in the New Testament. In all three of the synoptic gospels (Mt 3:13–17; Mk 1:9–11; Lk 3:21–22), the Holy Spirit plays an important role in Jesus' baptism. The heavens open and the Spirit descends like a dove, alighting upon Jesus as he arises from waters of the Jordan. A voice from heaven proclaims that Jesus "is my beloved Son, with whom I am well pleased" (Mt 3:17). Jesus' baptism can be seen, among other things, as his commissioning for the ministry he is called to undertake on his father's behalf. Indeed, Matthew carefully records this story so that the reader sees Jesus' baptism as a fulfillment of God's plans set forth in the Old Testament. Jesus is the one who will lead the restored community envisioned by Ezekiel into righteousness. And it is the Holy Spirit who provides the link between prophecy and fulfillment.

After a period of formation in the wilderness, where the Spirit leads him immediately following his baptism, Jesus is tested and proved ready for service. He returns to Galilee to preach and calls together his disciples. Here we see Jesus gathering a company of people who are instructed and empowered to take his good news of God's redemption to others. Although Scripture notes that Jesus did, on occasion, remove himself from the fellowship of his followers for a period of prayer (Mk 6:45–46) his life and ministry are carried on within that community. Jesus is not a loner. And after his death and resurrection, Jesus returns to his disciples to prepare them for receiving the same Spirit who marked the beginning of his ministry.

BABEL REVISITED

You may recall the story in Genesis about the unsuccessful attempts of the men of Shinar to build a city with a tower reaching up into the heavens (Gen 11:1–9). The writer makes a point of telling us that in that day everyone spoke the same language.

The motivation for building such a tower appears to be rooted in pride and disobedience, in the people's desire to make a name for themselves, to flaunt their power before God, and to challenge God's authority.

Yet forming a community for this purpose is not a good end and it understandably meets with God's displeasure. God thwarts their plans by confusing their language. Now they are no longer able to communicate with one another and they cannot continue building their city. Eventually they scatter across the face of the earth. Community cannot exist when people are incapable of understanding each another.

Another story in Scripture tells us how people are brought together when they are given the ability to speak a common language and are motivated by an end that, this time, pleases God.

After Jesus' ascension, the disciples await the fulfillment of God's promise to baptize them with the Holy Spirit. It is not clear from Scripture that they understand just what it is they are waiting for, but Jesus has told them that they are to be his witnesses to the ends of the earth and that the Holy Spirit will come upon them to give them power to do so. And indeed, as they wait and wonder, a day comes—while they are gathered together in one place—when an astounding event occurs. The disciples are startled by the sound of a mighty, rushing wind filling the room where they are praying. Suddenly, tongues as of fire alight upon each of them. They are filled with the Holy Spirit and begin to speak in the tongues of other languages.

The gift of the Holy Spirit immediately gives the disciples the ability to communicate with people of many nationalities despite the fact that they do not speak one another's language. When spoken under the guidance of the Holy Spirit, the language of faith becomes universal. Here we see just the opposite of Babel. The gospel is the common language that brings people together. It is the language that forms the foundation of Christian community.

When they realize the effect their utterances have on other Jews in Jerusalem who have come on a pilgrimage to the temple from far away countries, the apostles turn to Peter to be their spokesperson. He takes the initiative and addresses all those in the streets who will listen. Although Peter's native tongue is not one the pilgrims know, they all understand what he is saying. This uneducated fisherman now boldly speaks about Jesus Christ. He tells the crowds who gather around the apostles that Jesus, who was recently crucified and killed, has been raised up by God—triumphant over death—and that he and his fellow apostles are witnesses to this extraordinary series of events.

Scripture tells us that the hearers are "cut to the heart" (Acts 2:37). They want to know what they should do in response to Peter's impromptu sermon. Peter's response is simple and direct: "Repent, and be baptized every one of you in the name of Jesus Christ for the forgiveness of your sins; and you shall receive the gift of the Holy Spirit" (Acts 2:37–38). And so they do just that. That day 3,000 people are baptized as a result of hearing the gospel preached and they too receive the Holy Spirit. And the Spirit's effect is immediately felt. Afterwards those newly baptized people begin to bond together in fellowship. They gather with one another for worship and prayer and teaching. Furthermore, they decide to hold their possessions in common and share with others among them when anyone had need. The mistakes of Babel are not revisited upon this community, who are given voice by the Holy Spirit to speak to one another in the common language of the gospel.

INITIATION INTO CHRISTIAN COMMUNITY

Just as the Spirit of God hovered over the waters at the beginning of creation, so too the Spirit hovers again over God's new creation at Pentecost. We come to know this new creation as the "church"—the community of fellow Christians—the Body of Christ. God has given the Holy Spirit to the apostles so that they may draw other believers together through their preaching. The baptism of these new converts with water and the Holy Spirit leads to the formation of communities of believers in which one worships, finds fellowship, and is nurtured in the faith.

Throughout the Acts of the Apostles we hear how the apostles, singly or in pairs, preach the gospel to Jews in Jerusalem and the surrounding countryside, and later through Paul, to gentiles in distant lands. Generally the pattern of proclamation and reception is the same: first the good news is presented, then those hearing it desire to be baptized for the forgiveness of their sins. Upon their baptism with water and the Holy Spirit they become members of the growing Christian community. The Holy Spirit first enables preachers to speak and listeners to hear and then empowers those who are baptized to carry on the work of proclaiming the gospel and building the community.

However, there are instances in the Acts of the Apostles when people are baptized with water, but they do not receive the Spirit. Philip, the deacon, brings the good news up to Samaria, after the persecution of Christians begins in Jerusalem, and many ask to be baptized (Acts 8). But the Spirit is not poured out among them. When the apostles in Jerusalem hear that Samaritan Jews responded in faith to Philip's preaching, Peter and John make the journey up to them and pray for their reception of the Holy Spirit. We can gather that, as missionary activity now begins in earnest, it is necessary for apostolic representatives of the "mother" church or community to affirm this new community of Christians outside Jerusalem. By coming to lay hands on the believers in Samaria, Peter and John are, in effect, founding "the church" in the regions beyond the traditional Jewish homeland.* In other instances, people receive the Holy Spirit upon hearing the gospel proclaimed, without first being baptized with water. In the Acts of the Apostles, Peter is brought to the household of Cornelius, a gentile. Cornelius is desirous of hearing the good news offered by God through faith in Jesus Christ. Because the

---

* Aidan Kavanagh, *The Shape of Baptism* (New York: Pueblo, 1978) 19.

Christian community in Jerusalem had not yet taken up the issue of whether the gospel should be preached to non-Jews, Peter is faced with a dilemma, but God indicates to him through a dream that this is God's will (Acts 10:9–16).

No sooner had Peter laid out for Cornelius and his household the story of Jesus, crucified and risen, then the Holy Spirit descends upon them. Though they had not yet been baptized with water, the gift of the Spirit was confirmation to Peter that God desired these gentiles to hear the good news and become part of the Christian community. Exceptions to the usual order of baptism (water first, *immediately followed* by an outpouring of the Holy Spirit) seem to occur when God is leading the apostles to affirm a more expansive vision of God's church. Christian communities now include not only Jews beyond Jerusalem but gentiles as well.

Thus, what always follows the gift of the Holy Spirit— whether it is given before, during, or after baptism with water— is a gathering into community of those who already believe. And although the components of baptism sometimes occur in a different order and on separate occasions, it is the exception to the rule under unique circumstances. Baptism should always be seen as a single action—with water and the Holy Spirit—that follows the proclamation and reception of the gospel. The end result is the establishment and empowerment of communities of believers.

We see in Scripture how God decided in creation that human beings should not be alone. In the Old Testament, God called a chosen *people*. God spoke to a community. The laws and instructions given to Israel were given so that they could live *together* harmoniously. In continuing the precedent God had already established, baptism becomes the community-building sacrament that is instituted through the Holy Spirit in the aftermath of God's intervention in creation through the death, resurrection, and ascension of Jesus Christ. Therefore, one is not baptized to live apart from the community of faith. It makes no sense for parents to ask to have their child baptized if they have no desire to belong and share in the life and worship of a particular congregation. It flies in the face of God's post-resurrection plans for God's people.

Moreover, the Holy Spirit not only gathers Christians together, the Spirit also works to sustain and empower the groups in which Christians have congregated.

LIFE IN CHRISTIAN COMMUNITY

In the Acts of the Apostles, we are told that those who were baptized in response to Peter's preaching "were together and had all things in common; and they sold their possessions and goods and distributed them to all, as any had need. And day by day, attending the temple together and breaking bread in their homes, they partook of food with glad and generous hearts" (Acts 2:44–46). Clearly, the Spirit has had a powerful effect upon the new converts. Their desire for fellowship with one another and the selfless way that they looked out for one another's needs is truly remarkable.

This may lead one to think that life within the early Christian communities was always harmonious. Indeed, Christians today often have an idealized view of life in the early church, thinking of that time as "the good old days." The Holy Spirit did give the members of these new communities the ability to overcome the usual obstacles that arise when human beings attempt to live among one another so closely. But there were instances of conflict and division almost from the beginning. What is important to note is that human pride and selfishness cannot ultimately thwart the work of the Holy Spirit. The Spirit prevails in the end.

A man named Ananias, along with his wife Sapphira sold a piece of property and purported to give all of the proceeds from the sale to the fledgling church (Acts 5:1–11). However, what they neglected to say is that the amount given was not the entire sum from the sale. Instead, they kept a portion for themselves, which would have been fine if they had said that's what they were doing. They were not obligated to sell their land, and even when they did they were not required to give any of it to the Christian community. Others, however, had sold their possession of lands or houses "and brought the proceeds of what was sold and laid it at the apostles' feet [so that] distribution [could be made] to each as any had need" (Acts 4:34).

Ananias and Sapphira apparently wanted credit for the sacrificial giving of their possessions without actually having to be sacrificial. Their gesture was not only dishonest, it broke faith with their fellow Christians. When Peter confronted each of them separately about their deception, both were so overcome they collapsed and died. What this story tells us is that human nature is full of conflicting desires—to be self-serving and prideful as well as magnanimous and humble. Christians find themselves embracing virtues as well as vices just like anyone else and they will behave badly at times toward one another. But when they do so their selfish actions introduce death into the community. That is why Peter feels he must call into question the genuineness of Ananias and Sapphira's gesture right away. This is an example of Spirit-inspired leadership that insists members of the community be accountable to one another.

We also hear of tensions in the early church between two groups of Jewish Christians (Acts 6:1ff). The "Hellenists" were Greek-speaking Jews who had grown up beyond the biblical territory of Israel—in the Diaspora—who most likely had adopted some Greek customs. The "Hebrews" were Jews native to Jerusalem who had not been exposed to customs of non-Jewish cultures. The Hellenists protested that the Hebrews were overlooking some of their needy members. The apostles settled the argument by appointing impartial members to take over the responsibilities of looking after the widows in their midst—both Hellenists and Hebrews—who were in need of goods and services.

Furthermore, we are told that a great dissension arose

between Paul and the leaders of the church in Jerusalem, notably Peter and James, over the issue of evangelizing gentiles. Although Acts records the conflict as simply a difference of opinion that was settled quickly and amicably (Acts 15:1ff), Paul indicates that the debate was quite heated and an element of mistrust lingered even after a settlement was reached (Gal 2:1ff).

And certainly in Paul's churches there were a number of instances when members snubbed one another or tried to sue a fellow Christian in civil court. A cynical person might conclude that life within Christian community is no different than in any secular organization, with episodes of conflict and controversy, and that one is often better off not joining up.

Yet it is clearly God's desire that those who turn in faith to Jesus Christ be gathered together for worship and fellowship and mutual support. The Holy Spirit was poured out at Pentecost not only to empower people to proclaim the good news and to ensure that others would hear it, but also to initiate converts into God's new community, the church. God knows that it is at times difficult for human beings to get along with one another. God is fully acquainted with our nature. So the Holy Spirit serves to foster trust and goodwill among Christians so that we might overcome the selfish tendencies that draw us away from one another.

SALVATION IS FOUND IN THE CHURCH

We know that conflicts will occur. Some members may treat others with contempt. Sometimes people are deceitful. However, the Spirit can pour healing balm on our wounds. We can learn to forgive one another. We can help each other in the struggle to amend our lives. We can support our fellow members through difficult times and rejoice together during the good times. Christian community is where we can experience the presence of God—learning how to love as God does and to receive the love of God through fellow Christians.

Accordingly God has designed, through the gift of the Holy Spirit, Christian community to be the place where we can encounter a bit of heaven on earth through the grace of the sacraments and the sometimes sacrificial love and support of members. Through baptism each person is given gifts and talents to share with others in the community, to foster interdependence, and to accomplish the work that needs to be done on Jesus' behalf. Indeed, the Christian community needs to employ its accumulated strengths not only to maintain its own viability, but also to carry on Jesus' mission to the rest of the world. Each of us is given some gift that is needed by our fellow Christians, just as we are in need of their gifts. As Scripture tells us, some are given gifts to be prophets, leaders, teachers, administrators, helpers, healers (1 Cor 12:28).

Thus, through the Spirit, Christians are given the ability to sustain the kind of fellowship that had, in the past, eluded previous communities in the Bible. Therefore, we are not to seek the outpouring of the Spirit through baptism and then squander our blessing by refusing to belong to a community of faith. God did not intend for a Christian to worship alone.

It is helpful at this point to employ a phrase that formerly conjured up notions of damnation: Salvation is found in the church. This is useful only in the sense that it helps us to see that what we can most genuinely know about God we discover through belonging to a community of faith. Godly love, forgiveness, and empowerment are manifested through us and our fellow Christians, fallible though we all are. Yet together we are the church and what salvation is all about can be discovered in our midst.

Many people take the term "church" to refer to a building or an institution run by a distant hierarchy. But in New Testament terms, the church is a community, the Body of Christ. As the apostle Paul so eloquently argues, a body cannot consist of one person, or of a select few. A body depends upon all its members to function properly. So too, God calls upon all baptized persons, not to go it on their own, but to come together as the Body of Christ.

CHAPTER 2

BAPTISM IS ABOUT BECOMING A DISCIPLE

It may have appeared to some of Jesus' disciples—as well as to some of the Christians newly baptized after Pentecost—that being a follower of his was an illustrious designation. Certainly during Jesus' earthly ministry masses of people came out to hear him and in a number of circles he was esteemed as a great teacher. Perhaps being a part of his "entourage" at times felt quite grand, just as it may now for people who travel with a celebrity or a sports star.

It appears that James and John, the sons of Zebedee, were under such an impression. Even though Jesus had warned his disciples repeatedly about his impending degradation and death, his words fell on deaf ears. They could not foresee how Jesus could ever be rejected and put on trial as a common criminal. So instead, they looked forward to a time when Jesus would come into his kingdom, joyously hailed as the Messiah. In anticipation of that great day, they sought to position themselves for important roles in Jesus' administration, much like significant campaign contributors do with the winner of an election.

DRINKING THE CUP

In the tenth chapter of the Gospel of Mark, James and John make their request of Jesus: "Teacher, we want you to do for us whatever we ask of you...Grant us to sit, one at your right hand and one at your left, in your glory" (Mk 10:35, 37). In effect they are saying, "We want to be major players when you come into power." Jesus replies, "You do not know what you are asking. Are you able to drink the cup that I drink, or to be baptized with the baptism with which I am baptized?" They respond in the affirmative, without a clue as to what Jesus means. Had they known he was talking about his passion and death their answer would probably have been much different. Indeed, when Jesus was arrested and sent to trial all the disciples ran for cover. They had not anticipated such a calamitous ending to Jesus' ministry and they realized that their lives, too, were in danger.

It is not as though Jesus didn't try to prepare them for the consequences of being one of his followers. Far from being glamorous, life as a disciple is one of sacrifice and self-denial, for it is to be lived as Jesus lived his. However, the followers of other religious leaders were held in high regard, and Jesus' disciples probably assumed they would be also. They did not truly understand the social and political implications of Jesus' message, even though it was deemed subversive by the status quo. Jesus drove out the money changers from the temple, invited tax collectors to follow him, dined with notorious sinners, and often left the religious authorities looking like fools when they tried to trip him up. Therefore, following Jesus, imitating his way of life, was not only morally and spiritually rigorous, it was also a thankless and dangerous undertaking.

Other teachers and rabbis held places of honor in the community, as did their devotees. And certainly some deserved this respect. However, others set a very different example. We hear in the gospels how Jesus' contemporaries liked to call attention to themselves when they observed religious practices. They made a show of giving alms, so that others would be impressed by their generosity. They made sure people were watching as they offered elaborate prayers in the synagogues. They put on pious airs when they were fasting. Moreover, they were careful to keep God's laws—every one of them. They did so, not so much out of a love for God, but instead to secure the esteem of others. And finally, they were quite unkind to people who had been unfortunate enough to be born poor or sick. Sadly, men like these were role models for many people.

Jesus called his followers to live life quite differently. He encouraged them to break religious laws, if doing so actually meant they would more faithfully live up to what God had originally intended. For example, they were to treat those carefully avoided by the religious leaders—people of ill repute—with kindness and respect in the hope that such people would turn back to God. And they were to love their enemies, and pray for those who persecuted them. Again and again, Jesus tried to explain to his disciples that such behavior would only alienate them from the religious establishment and that they needed to be prepared for scorn, not admiration. His words largely fell on deaf ears.

Jesus' revolutionary teaching and actions ran counter to cultural assumptions of the day. It was universally assumed that those whom God had blessed were the well connected, the well heeled, and the healthy. Their success was surely evidence of God's favor. Yet Jesus taught that God is pleased with those who suffer on his behalf and that doing so may mean losing everything, including their livelihood and good name. Moreover, those who seek to store up earthly riches get no reward in the end. The blessed are those who devote their energy to proclaiming God's kingdom without concern for establishing a secure way of life on earth. Finding favor with God entails a high degree of humility and sacrifice that others may find odd and foolish. Therefore, family and friends would probably not be impressed with a decision to follow Jesus. In fact, a person may even have to choose between them and Jesus.

Jesus spent a great deal of time trying to help his disciples reorient their expectations and responses to life. What is valued in God's kingdom was often radically different from the social mores of their day. For example, when a dispute arises among the disciples about which of them should be regarded as the greatest, Jesus admonishes their behavior. It is a waste of God's time to be arguing over issues of rank and power. However, like middle managers contending with one another over who gets to use the executive restroom, the disciples each want to establish their own importance in ways the world understands. But in God's kingdom what is valued is one's willingness to serve. Rank is of no importance. Jesus uses that awkward moment to instruct them to be like him—even though he could claim executive privilege he is among them as one who serves (Mk 9:33–35; 10:41–45).

As he prepares to send his disciples to proclaim the good news of God's kingdom, Jesus tries to impress upon them the risk of such an undertaking. Some people will receive their witness with glad hearts, but others will seek their downfall. He tells them they are being sent as sheep in the midst of wolves. They will be delivered up to councils and flogged. They will be run out of town. His followers must be prepared for rejection, even death, for what is good news to some is threatening to others. Therefore, one must be prepared to sacrifice everything for Jesus' sake.

Jesus will have no part of a follower who is not prepared to suffer greatly in service to God: "Whoever does not bear his own cross and come after me, cannot be my disciple" (Lk 14:27). The cup that Jesus will drink, they must drink also. The baptism with which Jesus is baptized will be their baptism, too. Therefore, being a disciple means being prepared to die.

ALL THE BAPTIZED ARE DISCIPLES

Today the term "disciple" is probably not one the average Christian would use to define him or herself. Disciples are often thought to be quite zealous about their faith, not people who simply attend worship on Sunday mornings. In this light, a disciple is someone who goes to Bible study, undertakes a lay ministry, or is involved in a leadership position in the congregation or diocese. Others may say that a disciple is someone who is an exception to the rule—a person who is committed to learning more about faith and to participating in ministry. However at baptism we take vows to do just that.

We promise to follow and obey Jesus as our Lord (Appendix, 101) which means we will commit ourselves to studying God's word spoken to us through Scripture and the faith handed down to us from the apostles. We will offer ourselves for service in our church or in our community as representatives of our church. It means, in the words of the Baptismal Covenant, that we will "proclaim by word and example the Good News of God in Christ; and to strive for justice and peace among all people" (Appendix, 103). The implications of baptism are such that everyone is made a disciple. Therefore all of us are called to devote our lives to following Jesus, just as a disciple did in Jesus' time. Being a disciple is not the call of a special few within a congregation.

Yet we may find that we unconsciously assume that working at being a Christian means that we only focus on what we perceive our needs to be. We ask for God's assistance with the ups and downs of life; we open our hearts to receive God's blessings; and we fall into the habit of expecting God to be at our beck and call. In this way, living a Christian life can turn into a self-centered exercise of seeking our self-fulfillment. However, while it is true that God wants to heal us, strengthen us, and bless us, God does so in order to prepare us to be better able to serve him. God is not our servant; we are God's.

Service is what characterizes a Christian life. And in order to serve God, a baptized person must be willing first to be disciplined by him. The word discipline often has a negative connotation for people, associated as it is with the notion of punishment. However, many people would be surprised to know it is derived from the word disciple. Its primary meaning is to give instruction, guidance, and formation. God is the teacher and we are God's pupils. Being disciplined is actually about having one's life given shape in a particular, distinct way. All people who are baptized must let God discipline them so that they are ready to live a life of service as a disciple.

And, just as it was for Jesus' early followers, becoming a disciple is an unsettling procedure. Our expectations need to be realigned just as theirs were. And, we need to give Jesus our complete allegiance. Nothing or no one else can share our full loyalty and devotion. Jesus demands an obedience that is going to be costly at some point, perhaps even painful; it may engender conflict. Be aware: there is a price to be paid for being a disciple.

DYING TO OUR WILL

Jesus sums up the process of becoming a disciple by talking about death: "He who finds his life will lose it, and he who loses his life for my sake will find it" (Mt 10:39). Being baptized means we must die to whatever gets in the way of being faithful to Jesus. This is not an easy process. Dietrich Bonhoeffer, a Christian theologian and activist against Hitler during World War II, wrote a stunning book in 1937 called, *The Cost of Discipleship.* In it he writes: "When Christ calls a man he bids him to come and die...because only the man who is dead to his own will can follow Christ. In fact, every command of Jesus is a call to die, with all our affections and lusts."*

What Bonhoeffer is saying is that being a disciple is about dying to our will, dying to anything we may prefer over serving Jesus, dying to things and commitments that may compromise our complete loyalty to him. For Bonhoeffer it meant postponing his marriage and returning to Germany after arrangements had been made to shelter him in America. He could have grown old

---

* Dietrich Bonhoeffer, *The Cost of Discipleship* (New York: The Macmillan Company, 1963) 99.

with a devoted wife beside him and grandchildren around his table. He could have helped those leading the opposition back in Germany from a much safer distance on the other side of the Atlantic. But Bonhoeffer believed that being a disciple meant one must die to what may seem reasonable at the moment, but is not truly faithful in the end. Such discipline did literally cost him his life.

We, too, must ask ourselves some tough questions about commitments we have made, which we assure ourselves are quite reasonable, but actually, in light of the gospel, are not truly faithful. For instance: Is there anything that regularly diverts your attention from God? Is work something you use to feel better about yourself? Is the desire to get ahead making you ruthlessness? Are your long hours on the job ultimately serving God's kingdom or your own fear of either losing your job or your sense of identity and worth? If you have no time even to set aside and reflect upon this question of devotion, then you have some dying to do. In the end, we are ultimately to serve Jesus, not our self-esteem and not our boss.

FOR REFLECTION

Think about the way you use your resources—God's resources, actually. Although having nice things is not necessarily bad, a spiritual cost arises when we end up serving our need for status and possessions instead of serving Jesus. While it is certainly possible to be comfortable *and* faithful, true comfort comes from the Lord, not possessions.

- Do I spend too much time thinking about what I need to have next or how to maintain the lifestyle I currently have?
- How much effort do I put into acquiring and preserving?
- Is the status that comes with conspicuous consumption more important than the designation of being God's servant?

- What longings distract me from Jesus?
- Do I long to be comfortable or faithful?
- What do I trust in to give me comort?
- What about allegiances I have in the community—clubs, civic organizations, and fellowship groups? Do they ultimately serve God's purposes? Even if these groups or organizations are secular in nature, the work that is done falls under God's judgment.
- Would God be pleased with the goals and activities of these organizations?
- Do they unnecessarily hurt other people, even indirectly?
- Am I aware of all the ramifications of the commitments I have made within my larger community?

What may seem harmless and downright decent in polite company may actually have an underlying effect that is antithetical to the gospel. Perhaps the devil is in the details and you would rather not know. But no one can give allegiance to something that compromises, in any way, one's primary allegiance to Jesus. As Bonhoeffer said, every command of Jesus is a call to die, with all our affections and lusts.

The apostle Paul reminds us that baptism is a metaphorical death. He writes, "We know that our old self was crucified with him so that the sinful [nature] might be destroyed, and we might no longer be enslaved to sin" (Rom 6:6). Paul is saying that baptism is about dying to our own will—which can lead us to make compromises and commitments of convenience that are ultimately unfaithful—and embracing, instead, the will of God. As I said earlier, at our baptism we promise to follow and obey Jesus as our Lord. That does not mean following our own instincts about what is good. We must learn to recognize the natural tendency we have to choose what is safe and only appears, from our often-clouded perspective, to be a good thing. This is what we must die to. Then we are to prayerfully turn to God and ask for God's perspective, which is pure and without ambiguity, and seek what God is calling us to be and do. Baptism is the beginning of a death that must be ongoing in us.

In the early church converts being baptized were totally submerged in a pool of water three times: first, in the name of the Father, and then, of the Son, and finally, of the Holy Spirit. The effect of this triple submersion was so powerful that converts felt as though they had symbolically died in that water and emerged into a new life. They had left their own will at the bottom of that pool and embraced their Lord's as they came up out of it. The same is true for all of us baptized today, even if the submersion is only done symbolically at a font.

Martin Luther understood baptism to be a kind of death that needs to occur each day in the life of a disciple when he wrote, "A [baptism] signifies that the old Adam in us should be drowned by daily sorrow and repentance, and be put to death with all sins and evil lusts; and that a new man should daily come forth and rise, to live before God in righteousness and holiness for ever."* The "old Adam" represents our will untouched by God's regenerative grace. The "new man" is each of us who commits to seeking God's direction, rather than relying primarily upon our own instincts and inclinations.

Furthermore, Jesus himself had to die to his will in order to be obedient to God's. Had he settled for anything less it would have been ruinous for all of humanity. In Gethsemane he prayed, "not as I will, but as thou wilt" (Mt 26:39). And those who would follow after Jesus, must pray the same prayer.

BEING GOOD VS. BEING FAITHFUL

We must be careful that we do not mistake God's will for something *we* have decided is a good and noble pursuit. For instance, we may firmly believe that it is a good thing to help the

---

* Martin Luther, *Luther's Small Catechism* (Columbus: The Lutheran Book Concern, 1927) 24.

poor. Who would argue with such a decision? After all, we are exhorted throughout the Bible to do so. But, our notion of helping may be very different from God's. We may offer to serve a meal in a soup kitchen or raise money for a non-profit organization that assists the needy. We may gather up clothes and food for a needy family during the holidays. However, such efforts are often undertaken in a way that makes us feel better about ourselves— and causes us little inconvenience—but is humiliating to those who are the recipients of our generosity.

In the aftermath of a devastating flood in eastern North Carolina in 1999, numerous church groups donated food and clothing to those who had lost their homes and were staying in temporary shelters. A number of these people, poor to begin with, were now destitute. One group of church members arrived at a shelter with a van full of supplies, late at night, when the people had already settled in for the evening.

The monitors at the shelter asked the church group to unload their supplies in a storage area so that the shelter guests could avail themselves of them in the morning. But the church group wanted to videotape their members handing out supplies to the "needy" so they could show it to their congregation when they got back home. The people staying in the shelter had little choice but to comply.

Who benefited most from this gesture? It was extended at great expense to those who were the recipients of a "good" deed. It cost them their dignity. A *good* deed is one like this, one that is done completely on our terms. We are the ones who determine what to do and how to do it, in a way that is convenient for us. It costs us little. We do not open ourselves up to be transformed by our efforts. Instead we condescendingly hope our efforts transform others, so we can feel good about ourselves. On the other hand, a *faithful* deed, one done in accordance with God's will is a sacrificial enterprise. We give of ourselves humbly and expect nothing in return, finding perhaps even rejection. Our efforts are undertaken with the goal of glorifying God, not enhancing our own sense of beneficence. Left to our own devices, we have narrow assumptions of what God would have us do, because our ego gets in the way. And we manage to see to it that we risk little.

Jesus wants, first and foremost, to convert our will. He is seeking people who will be obedient to him. That way he can lead us beyond our convenient, safe, and self-serving choices so that we can make ones that are wholly faithful to God. This obedience is an unsettling process, for it invades our complacency and exposes our selfishness. We discover how tenaciously we have been resisting God's will being done in our lives, and we begin to understand for the first time what being faithful is all about. Hence, becoming a disciple entails learning to recognize God's voice and to listen to God's voice rather than our own.

EMBRACING GOD'S WILL

Our baptism is the beginning of a new life, seeking God's will as we continue to die to our own. Only then are we allowing Jesus the opening he needs to begin the transformation of our wants and desires into something more in line with Godly ones. None of this is to say that all of our desires are bad; rather it is to acknowledge that what motivates them is, often enough, rooted in selfish instincts. When we can acknowledge this truth about ourselves we give Jesus a foothold so that he can quiet our more self-serving impulses and awaken new selfless ones, disciplined to respond to God's will.

Over the centuries much has been written about learning to seek and embrace God's will. Spiritual guides—such as John of the Cross, Julian of Norwich, and C. S. Lewis—have addressed the need to surrender all aspects of one's life completely to God. They caution us that this is not accomplished overnight. Just when we think we have turned everything over to God, God will reveal some aspect of our lives that we have not presented to him for conversion. Yet we should not be discouraged by this prospect because surrender of the will is a lifelong undertaking. In fact, as long as we are alive, there will be more surrendering to do. Yet even so we will discover at the same time that God continues to make progress with us. As God does so, we will be set free, more and more to "live in the power of his resurrection," an expression found in the service of Holy Baptism (Appendix, 104).

The apostle Paul lived in the power of Jesus' resurrection. In learning to die to his will Paul was able to serve God in such a way that allowed him to endure taunts, humiliations, danger, attacks on his life, and the constant threat of failure. Since he was not concerned with serving his ego, he was free to risk everything, even his own life, for Christ. Paul understood he had been granted a new life in Jesus Christ—so that even though he would die— he too, as a result of Jesus' own death and subsequent resurrection, would live again, forever: "For if we have been united with him in a death like his, we shall certainly be united with him in a resurrection like his" (Rom 6:5). Therefore Jesus' resurrected life begins now for the disciple who is willing to begin dying to his or her own will. We too can face the dangers Paul did, even death, for the sake of Jesus Christ while being, at the same time, more fully alive than we have ever been.

THE PROGRAM FOR RECOVERY BEGINS AT BAPTISM

When we talk about becoming a disciple and learning how to die to our own wills in order to embrace God's, we are talking about a process. It begins with the realization that our wills often get in the way of authentic faithfulness throughout our lives. Jesus himself entered a process of formation after his baptism, when the Spirit led him into the wilderness. There the devil tempted Jesus to make choices that seemed to be harmless, perhaps even good at first glance, but that would have been ultimately self-serving. For forty days Jesus fasted and prayed to prepare for this test. When it was finished, he was ready to take up God's work of salvation—a work that required absolute obedience.

We too need to see ourselves in a process of formation. It begins at our baptism when either we or our parents and sponsors discover what it means to belong to the church and become a disciple. This process actually needs to continue throughout our lives, for there will always be new learnings for us, times when we are ready to embrace even more fully God's will, as well as times when we succumb to the temptation to seek only our own.

Like an alcoholic who knows he or she will always be in "recovery" so too will we be in a recovery program to allow God to address and transform the selfish side of our nature. Moreover, we will at times lose our way because we are constantly seduced by a culture that encourages us to indulge all of our wants and desires without regard for others. This ideology is diametrically opposed to the notion of seeking God's will instead of our own. So all throughout our life we need, as we vow in the service of Holy Baptism, "to continue in the apostles teaching, breaking of bread and the prayers" (Appendix, 103).

In preparing people for baptism, either their own, or their child's or godchild's, it is important to present these issues of belonging and discipleship and to help them see that they are called to spend the rest of their lives in formation within the community of faith.

CHAPTER 3

PREPARING FOR BAPTISM

The notion that some sort of preparation before baptism is necessary dates back to the very first baptisms after Pentecost. The first step involved hearing the preaching of the good news of salvation through Jesus Christ. Next, those who were "cut to the heart" by this proclamation were exhorted by Peter to "repent." Upon doing so they were baptized and joined other believers (Acts 2:37–41).

As Christianity spread as a result of the missionary efforts of the apostles, including Paul, a more involved procedure for preparing people for baptism evolved. The earliest documented details of such a process is found in the *Didache*. The full title is, *The Didache, or Teaching of the Twelve Apostles* and scholars believe it was compiled sometime in the second century. The first part consists of six chapters and is referred to as "The Two Ways." It deals with appropriate Christian moral conduct and was used as a catechism for those who were preparing to be baptized.*

AMENDMENT OF LIFE REQUIRED

Of the two ways, as referred to in the *Didache*, one is the way of life and the other the way of death. The way of life begins with

---

* Kirsopp Lake, *The Apostolic Fathers*, Vol. 1 (Cambridge: Harvard University Press, 1912) 307.

an instruction found in the gospels, namely to love God wholeheartedly, and then also, to love one's neighbor as oneself. We may recognize this as the golden rule. Further commands regarding love of enemies are similar to those found in the Sermon on the Mount. The *Didache* makes plain that there is a specific ethical way to live one's life. One must make very careful and deliberate choices for what is holy, chaste, humble, and generous. Not to be intentional in this way is to choose the way of death, the way filled with evil deeds and evildoers. One is cautioned not to associate with those who are immoral, lest one take up the same habits.

These instructions made it clear that a person needed to participate in a program of moral "re-formation" before baptism. Although the length of time for such a program is not proscribed, the intention, certainly, is that the person preparing for baptism be forced to examine closely the values they had appropriated from their culture. The candidate was required to relinquish values that were not in line with Christian ones. It appears that in these early years the instruction was primarily of an ethical, rather than theological, nature.

By the third century, not only was there a program for preparing candidates (known as catechumens) for baptism, a process had also evolved for determining the readiness of a new convert to Christianity to begin such instruction. In the *Apostolic Tradition of Hippolytus*, a series of questions is asked of the newcomer to the faith concerning their reasons for wanting to be baptized. Witnesses were required to be on hand to vouch for the person's moral character. If one was employed as a brothel-keeper, painter of idols, actor, charioteer, gladiator, pagan priest, prostitute, or magician, one needed to cease those activities and take up a more appropriate occupation. Soldiers had to take a vow not to kill. If one was accepted after such questioning, the candidate could expect his or her conduct to be examined regularly.

Then a three-year period of formation began, during which the catechumens received instruction, although the content is not described. This period could be shortened, if the candidate's demeanor and actions demonstrated a readiness to proceed. As the catechumens entered the last step in preparation for baptism, they were required to give an account of their conduct over the past three years: Had they honored the widows? Had they visited the sick? Had they done good works? Once again, witnesses were called to attest to their truthfulness. Only after this last round of character examination could a catechumen begin the final preparations for baptism.*

DOCTRINAL INSTRUCTION

It appears that Lent may have evolved, in part, as a time for the final preparation of those to be baptized at the Easter Vigil, which was when most baptisms were performed. An account exists written by Egeria, an abbess or nun who lived in the fourth century, of how those preparations unfolded for catechumens in Jerusalem. The following is an excerpt from her writings:

> Names must be given in before the first day of Lent, which means that a presbyter takes down all the names before the start of the eight weeks for which Lent lasts here, as I have told you. Once the priest has all the names, on the second day of Lent at the start of the eight weeks, the bishop's chair is placed in the middle of the Great Church, the Martyrium, the presbyters sit in chairs on either side of him, and all the clergy stand. Then one by one those seeking baptism are brought up, men coming with their fathers and women with their mothers. As they come in one by one, the bishop asks their neighbors questions about them: "Is this person leading a good life: Does he respect his parents: Is he a drunkard or a boaster?" He asks about all the serious human vices. And if his inquiries show him that someone has not committed any of these misdeeds, he himself puts down his name; but if someone is guilty he is told to go away, and the bishop tells him that he is to amend his life before he may come to the font.[+]

---

* Geoffrey J. Cuming, Hippolytus: A Text for Students (Bramcote Notts.:Grove Books, 1976) 15–17.

[+] Thomas J. Talley, The Origins of the Liturgical Year (Collegeville: The Liturgical Press, 1986) 174–175.

Egeria goes on to describe the daily schedule for instruction conducted by the bishop every day, from six to nine in the morning. For the first five weeks the Scriptures are studied. The bishop teaches the candidates about the resurrection and all things concerning the faith. Then for the next two weeks, they study the Creed. Just before Holy Week begins, each candidate, who is accompanied by a sponsor, recites the Creed for the bishop. The catechumens continue to fast and pray throughout that last week. At the Easter Vigil they will be baptized. However, their formation process will continue for a time after their baptism, when they receive instruction regarding the theological ramifications of the sacrament.*

One can conclude from the instructions laid out in the *Didache* and *Hippolytus*, as well as the account by Egeria, that in order to enter the initial stages of preparation for baptism a person had first to demonstrate the moral character befitting a follower of Jesus Christ. The past was not of concern, even if it was disreputable, as long as the person had taken steps to amend his or her life. Once accepted, the person could expect to spend up to several years performing works of charity, only then becoming eligible as a catechumen and beginning the final preparations leading to baptism.

By the fourth century, an additional step had been added to the process. Two months before baptism, after acceptance by the bishop, the person would participate in an intensive study of the Scriptures and doctrine of the Christian faith. Such a long and thorough program of preparation had evolved because it was thought that authentically Christian living was at odds with the surrounding culture. The convert consequently needed to learn how to see and respond to life differently, the way Jesus taught. And this re-visioning took time and practice. The culmination of this process led to a metaphorical death in the baptismal pool and subsequent rebirth into a new reality that was marked by humility, kindness, self-sacrifice, and generosity of spirit.

---

* E. C. Whitaker, *Documents of the Baptismal Liturgy* (London: S.P.C.K, 1970 2nd ed.) 42–43.

THE ACCULTURATION OF FAITH

The landscape of Christianity changed drastically when it became the religion favored by the Emperor Constantine during his reign in the first half of the fourth century. Before this time Christianity had been an often-persecuted faith, held by people who had vowed allegiance to Jesus Christ, a man perceived to be a failed revolutionary. They did so at the risk of their lives because they resisted giving allegiance to both emperor and the cultural norms of the day. During Constantine's reign, however, Christianity gradually became the cultural norm. Over the next hundreds of years, many people converted to Christianity, some not so much out of conviction, as out of expediency: if the emperor favors it, it is in my best interest to favor it also. Thus, for certain people it became a matter of convenience to hold the Christian faith.

Now, instead of Christianity being a sharp critic of the cultural mores of the day and advocating a way of life that espoused a very different set of values, it was becoming domesticated. For example, when they were baptized, Constantine's soldiers would hold the arm that held their sword out of the water. They did this so that they could feel they were free to continue to engage in war and kill on behalf of the emperor. Furthermore, careerism became a pursuit of some of the clergy, who vied for positions of power and wealth. And, as more and more people desired to be baptized, the strict standards and procedures that had been in place were relaxed. What had been a process taking several years was now completed in several weeks.

Dom Gregory Dix writes in *The Shape of Liturgy*:

> The pressure of a hostile world [had] sufficed to keep the standard of Christian self-discipline high. With the relaxation of this pressure after the peace of the church (Constantine's Edict of Milan in 313), there was a greatly increased danger of a lowering of the standard for the majority of Christians, despite the ascetic ardor of the devout. And in spite of the

care taken about the instruction of the catechumens and the insistence on their attendance at the catecheses, the great mass of conventional converts which was now flooding into the church was very apt to remain not more than half Christian in its unconscious assumptions.*

Christian values were no longer revamping the thoughts and actions of converts to the faith. Instead the values of the surrounding culture were beginning to weaken and corrupt the standards set forth by Jesus and his apostles. This is the dawning of what has been referred to as "civil religion," a set of beliefs that, far from challenging the mores of the status quo, actually serves to keep it in place. Today, no one would find that this brand of faith challenges any selfish or prejudicial inclinations. Instead, civil religion helps ease the daily transactions of life, for it is simply a matter of adapting good manners.

As political forces were changing the course of Christianity a shift was also taking place in theological circles. The church, which had seen itself as a community, gathered and empowered by the Holy Spirit, gradually became an institution that dispensed salvation. This radical change in ideology did not take place overnight. The sheer numbers of people throughout Europe and the Middle East who had converted to the faith over the years required that the administration of care and oversight become much more hierarchal. Understandably, authority grew centralized. And, in time, such "authorities" became "the church."

Simultaneously, a theological debate began as to the effects of sin and the nature of grace. Augustine, one of the greatest theologians in the history of Christianity, came to believe that human nature was inherently sinful: despite our best efforts we humans would always fall short in some way of the good that God created us to do. Such teaching was not only biblically sound, but it

---

* Dom Gregory Dix, *The Shape of Liturgy* (London: Dacre Press, 1945) 356.

was also psychologically astute. However, Augustine also reached the conclusion that there is an "original" sin, which was Adam's, that every human being inherited at conception. He held that this original sin was passed on to each succeeding generation, literally, through sexual intercourse and that it needed to be removed in order for one's salvation to be possible.

THE NOTION OF BAPTISM AS INITIATION FADES

At this point, baptism became the means for removal of this grievous stain, even though it was originally held that baptism washed away whatever sins one had accumulated. There had been no doctrine of an original sin, and when one sinned again after being baptized, one confessed and sought to amend one's life. The initial emphasis in baptism was not on cleansing, but on rebirth. With this subtle shift in theological teaching, baptism evolved into a means of avoiding eternal damnation. More and more people came to be baptized solely to ensure they would not go to hell when they died. Without a challenging program of preparation, baptism became simply an insurance policy, not the culmination of a process of reordering one's life. The focus of the church shifted from conversion and formation to absolving individuals from the effects of original sin.*

The rite of baptism itself underwent a very subtle, yet significant shift in churches in the West, but not in Eastern Orthodox churches. It was originally understood that the Holy Spirit was freely bestowed in baptism through the Spirit's volition; no one was specifically needed to invoke the Spirit. Gradually, however, a prayer for bestowal of the Holy Spirit became the responsibility of the bishop.

In the earliest years of life in the church, the bishop had simply anointed the freshly baptized with oil, as an affirmation of all that had taken place. However, by the fifth century this anointing

---

* Steven Ford, "The Place of Catechesis in the Early Church" (*Saint Luke's Journal of Theology*, June 1981, Volume XXIV, Number 3) 192.

was increasingly seen as the bestowal of the Spirit, something only the bishop could do. With the political acceptance of Christianity, more baptisms were taking place more frequently, and a bishop could not be present at every one. Therefore the practice of "finishing" the baptisms when the bishop was able to be present developed, out of which the rite of confirmation emerged. In time the Holy Spirit was no longer connected with baptism, only later, at confirmation did one receive the Spirit.*

So gradually, in the Western realm of Christendom, baptism shifted from initiation into a Spirit-empowered community of faith, following a process of preparation, to the doling out of grace to those who wanted to avoid damnation. The purveyors of such grace came to be recognized as "the church." Lay people were those who sought the agency of the church in time of need. Generally speaking, these latter assumptions about the nature of baptism and the identity of the church still exist today.

Thus there were a number of forces at play that led to a significant change in the way baptism was understood and administered. In the early days, when Christianity was a misunderstood and persecuted faith, no one questioned the necessity of an intensive program of preparation. The moral differences between the ethos of the surrounding culture and the values of Christian faith could not have been more striking. However, when Christianity was officially sanctioned by the Emperor Constantine, its values became increasing acculturated. And, as the liturgy of baptism itself was gradually transformed from a powerful metaphor for one's death and subsequent resurrection into a magical act that removed the threat of damnation, the notion of belonging and becoming a disciple ebbed away.

The prayer book revision of 1979 sought to restore the sacrament of baptism as a rite of initiation. The very first rubrics on the opening page (Appendix, 95) indicate what is afoot: "Holy

---

* Aidan Kavanagh, *The Shape of Baptism* (New York: Pueblo Publishing Company, 1978) 53. Discussion expanded during classroom lecture at Yale Divinity School, New Haven, CT, November 13, 1986.

Baptism is full initiation by water and the Holy Spirit into Christ's Body the Church....Holy Baptism is appropriately administered within the Eucharist as the chief service on a Sunday or other feast." The role of the Holy Spirit in baptism has been recovered and the sacrament itself is to take place when the community gathers for its primary service of worship, which would ideally be a celebration of the Eucharist. No longer is baptism seen as a private affair. Full participation by the congregation is appropriate and desired. The congregation itself has the final word as they welcome the newly baptized: "We receive you into the household of God. Confess the faith of Christ crucified, proclaim his resurrection, and share with us in his eternal priesthood" (Appendix, 107).

PREPARATION AND FORMATION NEEDED TODAY

However, although we have restored in our liturgy the understanding of baptism as initiation into the community of fellow disciples, we have not restored the presumption that one needs to be prepared for this momentous and life-changing event. It seems to be the assumption that, since children brought to be baptized have at least one parent who is baptized, they will be brought up to live out their faith actively involved in the life and worship of the congregation. Not only is this assumption erroneous, it is also dangerous.

Many baptized persons today are the inheritors of the form of civil religion that arose in the wake of the Constantinian peace. For them, "church" is the institution that dispenses the sacraments that they desire, not the Body of Christ of which they are integral members. Furthermore, baptism is understood as what makes possible their entry into heaven, not the beginning of a life of following the savior whose death and resurrection opened heaven to them.

Moreover, many baptized people have had little formation in the faith, apart from Sunday school, if even that. So we end up baptizing children of unformed parents who will not be likely to see the necessity of their children's formation. We can revise our liturgy all we want, but if we do not reform our practice of preparation, we will perpetuate a form of religion that is more about manners than faithfulness, and our church rolls will continue to be filled with people who are content to be "inactive" members.

Centuries ago the Christian community understood that when people converted to the faith they were embracing a very different ideology than the one to which they had been accustomed. New converts therefore needed time to be able to stand back and realize how radically different Christianity was from the mores of the culture in which they lived. They needed to develop habits of charitable service. And furthermore, a process of preparation was necessary to enable them to continue to live within society and resist temptations that would draw them away from God. An ongoing, lifelong process of formation after baptism was assumed.

We need to return to the understanding that preparation for baptism is necessary, and that it should be viewed as a process of conversion and formation. The dynamics of living in a pluralistic society today as a Christian are little different than they were during the time of Hippolytus and Egeria. For instance, our culture values appearance over than reality. It judges worth by material indications of success. It teaches us to love conditionally. It emphasizes personal convenience at the expense of the common good. It rewards selfish behavior and measures the worth of any relationship on the basis of what can be gotten out of it. The message we are given by these assumptions is that a human life is expendable. This is the ethos under which we live and work everyday, and we unconsciously buy into these values. In the end, there is little difference between the tensions the earliest Christians experienced while trying to live a faithful life and the ones we face. They lived in a pre-Christian society; we live in a post-Christian one.

The cultural values we may assume are Christian are not necessarily so. Instead, they are the values of a democracy: be honest, pay your taxes, respect the rights of others, and conduct yourself with decency. The gospel, if understood correctly, promulgates very different values: Be a servant to all. Forgive readily. Love unconditionally. Your worth is based upon God's love and not upon your achievements. The needs of the community come before your wants. Your resources belong to God and you are simply a steward of them. And finally, place God first in your life, before country, family, neighbor, and life itself.

The differences between an acculturated faith and the real thing could not be more disparate. The former advocates decency; the latter holiness. Decency does not require conversion of the will. In order to be decent, one must simply cultivate some manners. One can be selfish, yet respectable. Holiness on the other hand, necessitates surrender of one's preferences, habits, convictions—even one's identity—so that God can reshape them to be more in line with his. In order to be holy, one must seek to be obedient. The decent person may hold religious convictions; the faithful person is held by them.

Tolerance vs. Genuine Love

A recent article in a church publication told of a rector in California who decided to offer baptism to anyone in his town who desired it.* He calls this practice "open baptism." The rector placed an advertisement in a local paper inviting all who were interested to come to the Easter Vigil for baptism. The issue of membership in the church would be left up to each person's conscience. There were no classes to attend, no requirements to meet. Those who signed up for baptism received—by mail—a letter about the Easter Vigil service and two booklets explaining the sacrament.

---

* The Living Church, "With Open Arms," August 15, 1999, 15–16.

The rector believes his decision to baptize people regardless of whether they had—or desired—any church connection, without any kind of formal preparation is a witness to the gospel and the unconditional grace of God. He succinctly sums up the gospel as, "We fail miserably, but God loves us anyway." The rector believes that faith is a dynamic process rather than a momentary decision and that the process begins when people feel connected with a church. Then they are in a position to be nurtured in the faith.

There is something in his argument that appeals to members of mainline denominations. One could say that this rather unconventional method of reaching out to the unchurched or the unaffiliated speaks of acceptance and tolerance. It is not judgmental. It accepts people where they are. And certainly Jesus accepts people where they are—but he doesn't leave them there. He is ever calling us to a higher and deeper level of surrender and commitment to him. To sum up the gospel up as, "We fail miserably, but God loves us anyway," is to tell only half the story. God not only loves sinners, God calls them to a new life—a life we can only begin to live under the power of God's grace.

In our time, tolerance is the ultimate virtue. And being perceived as intolerant is an unforgivable sin. Yet we have confused tolerance with love. When we love someone we take them seriously enough to speak the truth to them. For example, Jesus says to the woman caught in adultery, "I do not condemn you; go, and do not sin again" (Jn 8:11). Jesus was not being tolerant. When one is tolerant, one chooses not pass judgment. When one loves, one passes judgment, but with truth and humility. Only then are we taking someone seriously enough to offer a perspective he or she may be blind to. Jesus did not condemn the woman. This is the gospel of grace. However, Jesus *did* define her conduct as sinful. This too is the gospel of grace. Grace only has usefulness when it is bestowed upon those who have fallen short. Therefore, talk of sin and grace go hand in hand. To speak of one without the other is to be less than truthful, therefore unloving.

A Christian community is meant to foster the kind of truthfulness that allows people to come to terms with their sins. And it does so when everyone is in touch with the fact that they are sinners. This way no one stands in judgment *over* anyone else. Everyone knows that they too fall short. The truth is told by people who understand the truth about themselves. This is love and this is what authentic Christian community is all about. Tolerance avoids such talk and the community that embraces tolerance doesn't really know what the gospel is all about.

When Peter preached to the crowds following the decent of the Holy Spirit at Pentecost, he mentioned both sin and forgiveness. Baptism is about proclaiming both of these to those who desire it. And doing so involves more than placing a welcoming ad in a local newspaper.

Furthermore, to say that church membership is up to a person's own conscience is to assume that someone already possesses the knowledge needed to reach a faithful decision. The early church understood that a conscience needs to be formed in how to think and act as Jesus would have us do. One didn't automatically know how to respond as a Christian. People needed some sort of basic preparation in what Christian faith is all about before baptism, so that their choices afterward would reflect a Christian view of the world, not a pagan one.

Thomas Talley writes: "Studies in the phenomenology of religion repeatedly demonstrate a rhythm of death and rebirth in rites of passage, a kenotic stripping away of status incumbencies as an integral part of the process of coming to a new identity.... Baptism, the radical conferral of new life in the risen Lord, includes, as integral to that new life, the renunciation of the old."* A person needs to understand that they espouse something that needs renouncing, before they can do so honestly.

---

* Thomas Talley, *Origins of the Liturgical Year* (Collegeville: Pueblo, 1986) 163.

Because so many people come to the church believing in a form of civil religion (which is nothing like the real thing), we cannot expect someone to be able to make a decision about something as important as church membership without some instruction, enabling them to make an informed decision. Reading a booklet or two is not enough. It takes personal contact and preparation from a priest or lay person who is not embarrassed to think he or she may know more about the faith than the person seeking baptism and has something important to offer. It may be that some clergy nowadays view baptism as a sacrament of welcome rather than a sacrament of initiation. However, since its inception at Pentecost, Christian baptism has always been the sacrament that receives one into the household of God. We can instead find a variety of creative ways to welcome people warmly to our churches. Indeed, there are a variety of ways—including advertising in the newspaper—to go out and *seek* people to invite to our churches. Nevertheless, in *The Celtic Way of Evangelism*, George Hunter suggests that we spend time building relationships with these newcomers and not rush them into making profound statements of faith.* Being ready to make such statements takes time and appropriate preparation and a willingness to seek to live into them within a Christian community.

So, by all means, we must accept people where they are, as they are, and welcome all who desire to be baptized, but we must also prepare them (or their parents, if they are young children) for what baptism entails: membership and discipleship. Not to do so grieves the Holy Spirit and does a disservice to the baptizands and the Christian community that welcomes them and vows to support them in their life in Christ (Appendix, 101).

---

* George G. Hunter III, *The Celtic Way of Evangelism* (Nashville: Abingdon Press, 2000) 99.

SECTION
II

This section is intended for use by small discussion groups, but it can also useful for private reflection. The following chapters provide material that is appropriate to cover in preparation for baptism, or for the reaffirmation of baptismal vows by individuals and congregations. I have outlined four sessions. However, if there are time constraints, sessions two and three can be condensed to form one session.

Minimal materials are needed: newsprint, tape, markers, Bibles, and Prayer Books.

The preparation described here only serves as a springboard, however, for a lifelong process of formation, within a community of fellow Christians. Many of the questions posed in these pages can be used again and again in this on-going process.

CHAPTER 4

COMPROMISED BY THE CULTURE

The first step in preparing for baptism is recognizing, if not welcoming, the challenges of living as a Christian in the twenty-first century. Like the earliest Christians, we need to take a hard look at the culture in which we live, and think about ways we may need to look beyond it in order to embrace more faithful living. This is a difficult task, best undertaken in the company of sister and brother seekers.

Parents who desire to have their children baptized (or adult candidates for Holy Baptism or the Reaffirmation or Renewal of Baptismal Vows) benefit greatly from a session or two of instruction that focuses upon some of the values our culture upholds that conflict with authentically Christian ones. Ideally this presentation and discussion would take place in a group of several sets of parents (or with a number of candidates for baptism, or for reaffirmation or renewal of vows), so that there is interplay, allowing for a lively discussion.

The following four sessions cover very basic material and lend themselves to an hour to an hour-and-a-half session.

The Context for Baptism: Then and Now

Pre-Christian Values

In pagan culture, social and civic functions were often held in the pagan temple, much like they are at a modern-day country club. Meat sacrificed to idols was regularly served. It was an accepted practice to engage in sexual relations with a temple prostitute.

Although Christians did not need to feel they had to withdraw from participating in society, some of these old habits needed to be questioned and curtailed. While it was common practice to gather at the pagan temple for various events, Christians were to avoid such occasions, even though it could mean they would lose their social position. New converts had to be prepared to accept this sacrifice.

Christians were called to look at the world very differently. For Christians, sexual relations between a man and woman were sanctioned—in fact, esteemed—if they were married to one another. Sex was understood as a sacred part of marriage, whereby the wife and husband become one in a mystical union. It was and is something very holy. One could only join oneself in this way to one's spouse.

Class distinctions were very carefully drawn in pagan culture. The wealthy and well connected were afforded privileges that the poor were not. No one questioned this. However, within the Christian community the classes mixed. The good news was heard and accepted by those in the upper classes as well as those in the lowest ones. Segregation of the classes would have undermined everything the gospel stood for. Therefore, everyone had to be willing to accept the fact that all were to be treated equally before the Lord. Although they might still continue to view one another as unequal when they conducted their secular business, when they gathered as a Christian community, all inequalities had to be checked at the door.

Christians also needed to learn to regard their leaders in a different light than their culture did. Humility and self-sacrifice characterized Christian leaders, while vanity, pomposity, and egotism characterized some pagan leaders. In fact, in pagan society, reputed authority figures were expected to call attention to themselves, to demand special privileges, and to develop a cult of followers, much like our modern day celebrities and sports heroes. This is how they earned respect. Christians had to learn to seek and esteem very different qualities in their leaders.

New converts to Christianity discovered that they were expected to embrace a very different set of values, values that their families, neighbors, and business partners would think ridiculous. They had to learn to be prepared to handle the inevitable tensions that would arise as a result of their commitment to follow Jesus Christ. This religious conversion would touch every aspect of their life.

POST-CHRISTIAN VALUES

Now, two thousand years later, is it any different for us who choose to follow Jesus Christ? Is not our culture often at odds with authentic Christian virtues? Let's think about this for a moment. How much do the values of the marketplace shape our understanding of ourselves and dictate how we relate to one another? Advertisers advise us, "Go ahead, buy our product, because you deserve it." Or better yet, "There are only two kinds of people in this world, those who own our product and those who only wish they did." These ploys tap into our baser instincts, and we often find ourselves espousing them. We are encouraged to buy a product because it is exclusive (a home in a gated community), or because it grants us a kind of status (name-brand athletic shoes), or because it helps to define our social position (a luxury car). We have been led to think of our possessions as extensions of ourselves. Therefore we can achieve self-esteem and the regard of our peers by buying bigger and better goods.

Indulgence and self-absorption characterize contemporary attitudes. We see these values at play in homes all across America when, for example, spouses contemplate leaving their marriages because they don't perceive the relationship to be fulfilling enough. It does not occur to them to reflect upon what they give to the marriage, as much as they reflect on what they are not getting out of it. Marriage is a school of sacrifice where each spouse seeks to place the needs of the other first, where their spouse's happiness leads to their own.

Parents like to think that they are placing the needs of their children ahead of their own, yet how often are they are motivated by self-serving instincts? Some parents sacrifice a great deal in order to provide extracurricular and self-improvement opportunities for their children, but there may be times the child would be better off simply spending more time with the parent. Buying the time of someone to teach our children skills is not necessarily a sacrifice. Perhaps it is an excuse for not giving more of ourselves.

Some parents push children to participate in various enrichment programs so that they may acquire an advantage over their peers. Self-improvement becomes a competitive sport, rather than a means of developing one's potential for the good of the world. A child may be driven by parents to excel in order to beat out others for a place in a good school, to go on to land an exclusive position in order to earn lots of money to be able to buy more and more goods. The values of the market are pervasive.

Marketplace values tell us that advertising does no harm, that it does not influence the way we regard the worth of people in our culture. Concerns to the contrary are dismissed with the argument that if one doesn't like the way a particular product is promoted one may simply choose not to buy it. Furthermore, we are often led to think that if a product makes money, there must be some good to it.

We are encouraged to believe that the ends justify the means. For instance, a company may compromise product safety or find an excuse to fire employees nearing retirement in order to save money and end up enjoying its best earnings quarter ever. The stockholders are pleased, so what is the problem? A political campaign may be filled with groundless innuendo and negative advertising, but our candidate wins. That's what is important, isn't it? The logical conclusion is that having scruples may get in the way of attaining our goal, and, in the end, winning is everything.

Personal convenience is paramount these days; we have come to elevate it ahead of the needs of others. We see this in action when someone is dangerously thoughtless and even rude to another person who gets in the way, whether it is while driving on the road or in a line at a grocery store. We are loath to impose limits upon our own freedom for the sake of others. We sometimes have difficulty functioning as a community, whether it is secular or religious, because we are unwilling to sacrifice for others. We form special interest groups to see that our needs are met, without necessarily having regard for the common good.

Many Christians have unthinkingly embraced these values. We bring them into play when we gather as a Christian community. We pass them on to our children. Therefore, just as the early Christians found it essential to spend time with new converts helping them to look critically at certain cultural assumptions, so too must we help those who are preparing for baptism, either their own or that of their child or godchild, or who are reaffirming or renewing their baptismal vows step back and evaluate how our culture has shaped their thinking.

SESSION ONE

HOLY BAPTISM IN THE THIRD CENTURY

Given our awareness of the similarities between our present society and that of the earliest Christians, we may find an exploration of baptism in the early centuries of the church instructive and more immediate than we might expect. The following excerpt is an adaptation by the Right Reverend Theodore Eastman of a third-century baptismal service recorded in the *Apostolic Tradition of Hippolytus*. It vividly portrays the way in which baptism symbolizes death and resurrection.

It is well before dawn on the first day of the week in Rome in the spring of a year in the first decade of the third century. Somewhere in the distance a rooster crows to announce the approach of the sun's first rays. Individuals and small groups of people move through shadowy streets toward a large house that has been converted into a place of worship.

Inside a small band of believers has been meeting for several days with a larger group of people who are preparing to become Christians. The catechumens, as the recruits are called, have been in training for three years. They have been tested in every way about the quality of their faith. They have attended corporate worship regularly, always sitting apart from those already baptized, always being dismissed after hearing the word proclaimed but before the bread is broken and the wine shared.

During the final phase of their preparation the catechumens have experienced the stiffest personal examination yet. Their piety, their understanding, their works of mercy have all been carefully scrutinized. The last examination is always done by the bishop himself. On Thursday night before the dawning Sunday the catechumens bathed themselves as a sign of their readiness. On Friday and Saturday they fasted and prayed. In an all-night vigil on Saturday night they listened to Scripture and other pious readings, and periodically the bishop said prayers of exorcism over each individual to dispel any remaining evil sprits.

As dawn now breaks the congregation is assembled in the main room of the house church. In another place, most likely in the garden with its pool and running fountain, prayer is said by the priest over the water. The candidates for baptism remove all of their clothing as a sign of leaving their past ways behind. Children are baptized first, speaking for themselves if they are able; otherwise parents or other relations answer for them. Male candidates are next, followed by women catechumens.

The baptismal ritual takes this shape. The priest anoints each candidate with "the oil of exorcism," previously blessed by the bishop. Then the priest asks if the catechumen believes in the triune God. After confessing faith in each person of the Trinity, the candidate is completely submerged in the water—three times in all—and then is anointed with "the oil of thanksgiving." Each new Christian is dried, vested in fresh white garments and brought into the main body of the church. There the bishop lays hands on each one [and] prays...and does a final anointing with "the oil of thanksgiving." The neophytes take their place with the rest of the faithful and all exchange the peace.

Immediately the congregation proceeds to the Eucharist, which includes not only bread and wine but also a mixture of milk and honey as a sign to the new Christians that God's promise to Israel has been fulfilled in the death and resurrection of Jesus Christ. These new Roman Christians fully understand that they have participated in the death and resurrection of Christ through their baptism, for they recall the powerful image that the great St. Paul used in the letter he wrote to the church in Rome a hundred and fifty years before. They have heard it read and reread many times.

The service is completed. The Christians return to their homes or to their jobs taking care not to attract too much attention. Forces in Rome are still very hostile to this new and different religion.*

How radically different the service of baptism was eighteen centuries ago. Not only was the liturgy itself quite unusual from our modern perspective—with complete submersion in water

---

* A. Theodore Eastman, *The Baptizing Community* (New York: The Seabury Press, 1982) 13–14.

and the donning of new white clothes afterwards. The intensive period of preparation beforehand is striking; three years is a long time, by any standard, to spend in study and training. Yet the early church understood that in being baptized, one was converting from one way of viewing the world to a completely different one. One's basis of reality was dramatically changing. Old assumptions, values, and habits needed to be re-examined. Christianity demanded that one give complete allegiance to Jesus Christ. It took time to be able to recognize how the mores of one's culture could be in conflict with Christian standards. And the newly baptized person needed the training and the knowledge to learn to cope with such a radical shift in ideology.

We have seen why the early Christians believed in the necessity of a prolonged period of preparation. The values of pre-Christian society were, in many ways, equally at odds with Christian values as the post-Christian society of the twenty-first century. It is useful to think about, in concrete terms, some of the assumptions inherent in our society and how they fit into a Christian worldview.

FOR DISCUSSION

The following is a two-part exercise. The moderator will need markers and several sheets of newsprint prominently displayed. In Part 1 of the exercise, write in a column the values espoused by contemporary culture that are articulated in answers to the following questions. For example, any number of commercials for beauty products stress the PRIMARY VALUE OF EXTERNAL APPEARANCE.

Part 1
1. Talk about the commercials we see on television. What are they telling us about our priorities as a culture?
2. Have you ever felt judged by others in regards to your wardrobe, your house or neighborhood, your car, your job,

your salary? Have you ever judged someone else in the same way? What leads us to do so?

Part 2

Read as many of the following passages from the Bible as time will allow. After each passage ask the following questions: Can you sum up the essential Christian value(s) depicted? What would our culture think of this? How would this be countered? Record the answers in the second column.

For example: "In everything do to others as you would have them do to you; for this is the law and the prophets" (Mt 7:12) tells us that we must regard all others—without exception—with the same FAIRNESS, KINDNESS, and PATIENCE that we deserve ourselves. It is *not* about good manners—being nice to those who are nice to you!

A dispute also arose among them as to which one of them was to be regarded as the greatest. And Jesus said to them, "The kings of the Gentiles lord it over them; and those in authority over them are called benefactors. But not so with you, rather the greatest among you must become like the youngest, and the leader like one who serves. For who is greater, the one who is at the table, or the one who serves? Is it not the one at the table? But I am among you as one who serves." (Lk 22:24–27)

Someone in the crowd said to him, "Teacher, tell my brother to divide the family inheritance with me." But Jesus said to him, "Friend, who set me to be a judge or arbitrator over you?" And he said to them, "Take care! Be on your guard against all kinds of greed; for one's life does not consist in the abundance of possessions." Then Jesus told them a parable: "The land of a rich man produced abundantly. And he thought to himself, 'What should I do, for I have no place to store my crops?' Then he said, 'I will do this: I will pull down my barns and build larger ones, and there I will store all my grain and my goods. And I will say to my soul, 'Soul, you have ample goods laid up for many years; relax, eat, drink, be merry.' But God said to him, 'You fool! This very night your life is being demanded of you. And the things you have prepared, whose will they be?' So it is with those who store up treasures for themselves but are not rich toward God." (Lk 12:13–21)

Then Peter came and said to Jesus, "Lord, if another member of the church sins against me, how often should I forgive? As many as seven times?" Jesus said to him, "Not seven times, but, I tell you, seventy-seven times." (Mt 18:21–22)

Jesus said, "When you give a luncheon or a dinner, do not invite your friends or your brothers or your relatives or rich neighbors, in case they may invite you in return, and you would be repaid. But when you give a banquet, invite the poor, the crippled, the lame, and the blind. And you will be blessed, because they cannot repay you, for you will be repaid at the resurrection of the righteous." (Lk 14:12–14)

All who believed were together and had all things in common; they would sell their possessions and goods and distribute the proceeds to all, as any had need. (Acts 2:44–45)

When the Lord your God has brought you into the land that he swore to your ancestors, to Abraham, to Isaac, and to Jacob, to give you—a land with fine, large cities that you did not build, houses filled with all sorts of goods that you did not fill, hewn cisterns that you did not hew, vineyards and olive groves that you did not plant—and when you have eaten your fill, take care that you do not forget the Lord, who brought you out of the land of Egypt, out of the house of slavery. The Lord your God you shall fear; him you shall serve, and by his name alone you shall swear. (Deut 6:10–13)

Part 3

Review the two lists and discuss the following questions.

1. Is it easy to live and work true to one's faith?
2. In what ways may our faith be compromised day to day?
3. How does one find the strength and support to live faithfully each day?

ON-GOING FORMATION OF ADULTS

"And they devoted themselves to the apostle's teaching and fellowship, to the breaking of bread and the prayers."
(Acts 2:42)

The early Christians understood that they needed to be in an ongoing program of character formation in order to remain true to Jesus Christ and the life he was calling them to live. The pressures to conform to their culture were so strong that they developed lifelong habits that would enable them to resist the daily temptations they encountered. The above passage from the Acts of the Apostles suggests that these habits involved study of Scripture and the Creed, regular attendance at the Eucharist, a discipline of prayer and fellowship with other Christians.

FOR DISCUSSION

1. What are you doing (or what might you do) to find strength and support to live faithfully every day?
2. Do you attend to your need for ongoing Christian formation?
3. Have you developed habits similar to the one's just described? If not, can you imagine how you might develop them?

Baptism entails obligations. Parents—as well as godparents—vow by their prayers and witness to help the child about to be baptized grow into the full stature of Christ. (Appendix, 100) This means that in order to raise children who will embrace Christian values parents or sponsors should first to be sure they are living them out faithfully.

However, we cannot live a Christian life on our own. We need other Christians to guide, support, and encourage us. We need to worship regularly in order to be reminded that God is our creator; that we did not create ourselves. We need to be challenged by Scripture and the teachings of the church. In fact, we vow to do all this every time we renew our Baptismal Covenant. (Appendix, 103)

ON-GOING FORMATION OF CHILDREN

We all know the pitfalls of raising children in this electronic age. As parents or sponsors, we are required to see to the Christian formation of our children and godchildren. To do that, we must be aware of the world our children live in.

FOR DISCUSSION

Moderator: Put out fresh newsprint and list the answers to the following questions.

1. What influences, attitudes, or authorities do you think will compete with you to interpret the world to children as they grow up?

2. What messages about life and human worth do they broadcast to our children?

3. In what ways are these messages either helpful or harmful?

HOW DO I CONTRIBUTE TO THE CHRISTIAN FORMATION OF MY CHILD OR GODCHILD?

All of us want to see to it that our children are shaped by morals and standards that are authentically Christian. In the service of Holy Baptism parents and godparents vow to "be responsible for seeing that the child [they] present is brought up in the Christian faith and life" (Appendix, 100). The following list contains but a few suggestions how we can accomplish this. As you read through this list, you may wish to discuss practical ways to incorporate these suggestions into your life. You may also wish to address the topic of what gets in the way or how you find the time.

- Begin by building a strong religious life within the family at home.

- Develop the habit of praying together as a family.

- Spouses should work on building a prayer life of their own together. Daily Devotions for individuals and families are offered in Book of Common Prayer beginning on page 136.
- Set simple goals in regards to developing a common prayer life.
- Read Bible stories to your children. Do it together as a family. After all, Bible stories are actually the family stories of our forebears in the faith. The goal is for children to come to think of them as stories about a family they belong to.
- Sing children's hymns together. Do this playfully throughout the day with little children.
- Encourage your child to develop a personal relationship with God. Help the child to see that God is intimately and actively involved in everyone's life; that God is concerned with our concerns.
- Develop the habit of praying with your child to God about his or her problems. This can be done at the end of each day, after school or after hearing or watching some disturbing news.
- Take that time to pray with your child both about issues that matter deeply to him or her as well as for things that occurred during the day for which they are thankful.
- Encourage your child to pray for the needs of others.
- Discuss what a Christian should do in certain situations that may occur in school—such as cheating, peer pressure, bullying—or in other contexts.
- Can you add your suggestions to this list?

It is important for parents to recognize that Christian formation and education takes place at home, not just once a week at Sunday school. Sunday school can only reinforce what is already being taught and modeled at home. It is never too early for children to learn that being a Christian, a disciple of Jesus, requires effort and sacrifice and may prove costly. Show by your example what living faithfully is all about.

BUILD A STRONG RELIGIOUS LIFE FOR THE FAMILY AT CHURCH.

Help your child to understand that your church is as much a "home" as the place that the family lives. Children should feel that church is a comfortable, safe, and familiar place, so that they are eager to spend time there. If you and your family go to your church regularly for worship, study, and fellowship your child will come to welcome spending time there. Children carefully observe their parents' habits. If you do not attend church functions regularly, your child will not be inclined to want to do so either. So you must set a good example. Your child will learn to imitate the example you are setting.

The child who grows up going to church and feeling good about the experience is more likely to turn to a church community in adult life, even after dropping out for a while.

LAY THE FOUNDATION

Parents must build this foundation early in life and be consistent. If participation in the church community has not been a family priority, parents cannot suddenly decide, when their children approach adolescence, that it would be a good thing for them to be involved in a church youth group and expect them to agree. A child's interest or lack of it will only reflect what they have learned from their parents' behavior.

Involve extended family members in important moments in your child's religious formation, such as Baptism, First Communion, Confirmation. Show your child that relatives and friends honor these moments.

SESSION WRAP-UP

Discuss Christian education programs for adults and children in your parish. If feasible, the moderator might lead a tour of the facilities for participants unfamiliar with them.

SUGGESTIONS FOR FURTHER READING*

PAMPHLETS⁺

"Family Prayer"
"Home Prayers for Little Children"
"Teaching Children to Pray"
"What Can I tell my Children About God?"

BIBLES AND BIBLE STORIES

Baker, Carolyn Nabors. *The Beginner's Bible for Toddlers.* Dallas: Word Publishing, 1995.

V. Gilbert Burns. *The Toddlers Bible Library*, Wheaton, Illinois: Educational Publishing Concepts, 1993. A series of individual books of biblical stories.

Ann Pilling. *The Kingfisher Children's Bible.* New York: Kingfisher Books, 1993. For children of all ages.

Ingram, Kristen Johnson. *Bible Stories for the Church Year.* San Francisco: Harper & Row, 1986. For pre-school and elementary-aged children.

HYMN RESOURCES

Pamela Conn Beall and Susan Hagen Nipp, eds.*Wee Sing Bible Songs.* Los Angeles: Price/Stern/Sloan, Inc., 1986. Tape/cd/booklet. Excellent songs for children of all ages.

---

* This list is by no means exhaustive. Parents and moderators are encouraged to add their own suggestions.

⁺ All available from Forward Movement Publications.

CHAPTER 5

WHY WE NEED A SAVIOR

Now it is time to examine the service of Holy Baptism more closely. If there are time constraints, sessions two and three can be combined into one.

SESSION TWO

A series of questions is asked of the candidates for baptism, if they are old enough to speak for themselves, or of their parents and godparents, if they are not. The first three questions have to do with our renunciation of the forces that work against God's purposes in the world. Ultimately, these questions ask us to acknowledge the presence of sin in our lives and in the world—sin generated by us and by other people and entities—and the various ways we succumb to or collude with it. This seems straightforward enough. However, people often misunderstand the notion of sin. And in order to come to some understanding of why it was necessary for God to go to the extreme of giving up his life for us, we need to come to terms with what sin is and how we are powerless over it.

THE LESSON OF ADAM AND EVE

We see sin enter the world through the story of Adam and Eve in the Book of Genesis. God gave Adam permission to eat freely of every tree in the Garden of Eden, forbidding only the fruit of the tree of the knowledge of good and evil. If Adam ate of this tree, he would die. The story makes clear that Adam is subordinate to God, his Creator. God can sanction certain activities and forbid others. We learn quickly that Adam is not willing to live within the boundaries of this relationship.

The serpent tells Eve that eating from the tree of the knowledge of good and evil will lead not to death, but to the kind of wisdom and insight that God alone possesses. The serpent asks why she and Adam should not be like God? Why should they have to continue living in a way that only points out the unequal nature of their relationship with God? Why can't they be on equal footing with God? Adam and Eve eat of the fruit of that forbidden tree.

As a result, they do gain insight, but this insight is of a most disquieting nature. For the first time, they see themselves as they truly are—mortal and vulnerable. Before, under God's benevolent protection, they were spared the awareness of the meaning of mortality, now they see only too clearly its consequences: their literal and figurative death. Now they will experience sickness, pain, frustration, and conflict. Before their quest to be like God, they were protected by God's blessings and goodness. God's love could conquer all things. By their action they opened a gulf between themselves and God, and nothing can bridge it. They are defenseless against the assault of mortality. And they alone are responsible for their terrible new awareness.

There seems to be a universal tendency in human beings to want to be like God, though chances are we don't express it quite so blatantly. We tend, for example, to want to see ourselves as at the center of a universe that revolves around us instead of one that revolves around God. We do not like to view ourselves as subordinates, even to God. Indeed, pride is the universal sin.

The story of Adam and Eve suggests that we stubbornly want to control life and the world around us, even though our attempts to do so only lead to more manifestations of sin: domination, manipulation, and obfuscation.

For Discussion

1. Do you agree with this analysis of the Adam and Eve story? Why? Why not?
2. What do you think this story tells us about human nature?
3. Can you think of examples in our culture that illustrate human pride and its consequences?

What is Sin?

We tend to think of sin in terms of individual actions and their consequences. However, our goal is to try to think beyond a *list* of sins in order to recognize the *propensity* to sin shared by all human beings. The specific sins one commits are simply a reflection of this universal disposition.

Those three questions for the Candidate or the Candidate's sponsors, known as the "renunciations" (Appendix, 101) point to an orientation, a motivating factor for our misdeeds, rather than the sins themselves. Therefore, when it is stated that we are all "sinners," the term is describing our *nature* rather than specific misdeeds or actions. To be human is to be a sinner.

For Discussion

1. How would you define or describe sin?
2. What is the difference between a sin and a propensity to sin?
3. Why is it important to understand the difference?

WE ARE NOT ALONE

The apostle Paul talks about this "condition" in his letter to the Romans. He writes, "I do not understand my own actions. For I do not do what I want, but I do the very thing I hate...I can will what is right, but I cannot do it" (Rom 7:15, 18b).

Perhaps you have struggled to be patient with someone who tries your patience dearly—a co-worker, a neighbor, a parent or child—vowing not to lose your composure the next time you are tested, only to discover that despite your best intentions you lose your temper again? Or perhaps you have struggled to overcome an addiction or unhealthy habit, but your resolve crumbles?

Everyone has experienced this frustration. Even our best efforts go awry. We often make a mess of things despite our good intentions. Who doesn't begin each day with great willpower and determination, only to fall short. And sometimes we can't even get to the point of having either willpower or good intentions. Perhaps we would all like to think that we are capable of mustering the will to be good and decent people all the time, pure of heart and mind, and that our sins are simply an indication that we have just not tried hard enough. However, Paul is endeavoring to tell us that even the most holy among us will inevitably fall short. In fact, it may be as it was in his case, that we sin precisely because we are prideful in thinking we are able not to.

FOR DISCUSSION

1. What is Paul saying in the letter to the Romans quoted above?

2. Can you think of a recent example from your own life when you have struggled like Paul?

WE ARE ALL EQUAL IN THE EYES OF GOD

No one can claim that they are more worthy before God than another. Flannery O'Connor perfectly captures the smug self-righteousness that may blind us from this truth in her famous short story, "Revelation."* The central character, Ruby Turpin, is a stout, middle-aged woman who does not hesitate to describe herself as a "good Christian woman." She means by this that her clean living, self-respect, and good manners make up for any shortcomings she may have. She honestly believes that she is more worthy of heaven than some other people she knows who live notorious lives or who are slovenly and rude. However, in the end, Ruby learns painfully that she is no better at heart than all the people she thought would never make it into heaven.

It was St. Augustine who concluded that we are *all* unable not to sin. One person may have more self-control than someone else, however, we all share in the fact that our basic motivations are never completely pure. Consequently the frequency and severity of our sins becomes irrelevant. We can never overcome, on our own, the universal tendency to choose self over God.

This also means that it is impossible for any of us ever to atone for our sins. We lack the purity of heart and mind. All our noble endeavors, even those done with a spirit of generosity and selflessness, are compromised in some way, however small. For example, there are people who possess a worldwide reputation for doing good deeds, people we sometimes refer to as living "saints." When she was alive, Mother Theresa was just such a person. Yet someone like this readily admits her own shortcomings. The outsider sees the good works. However, the person who is doing the work is well aware of her own inner struggles. Good is often done despite motivations that are not completely unadulterated. We should not hesitate to undertake such efforts, but we should

---

* Flannery O'Connor, "Revelation," *The Complete Stories* (New York: Farrar, Straus and Giroux, 1971) 488–509. Reading this story as a group would be a rewarding (and entertaining) exercise.

remain mindful that the doing of them will not change the fact that we are incapable of atoning for our sins. It is important to grasp this point and to remind ourselves of it as part of our on-going formation.

A GOD OF JUSTICE

Unforgiven, a 1992 film starring Clint Eastwood may shed some light on this issue of atoning for our sins. Eastwood's character William Munny, once a notorious thief and bounty hunter, gave up his rough and ugly life when he married his beloved wife. As the film opens, he is a widower, struggling to make a living as a farmer out West in the 1800s.

One day a novice bounty hunter, barely out of his teens, who calls himself, "The Schofield Kid," shows up on Munny's doorstep. He tempts Munny to join him in finding and killing a crazed cowboy who has slashed the face of a prostitute. There is a great deal of money, raised by the prostitute's associates, riding on the cowboy's head. Munny struggles with this unwanted temptation. He had promised his wife he would never return to his former ways. But with her death, a light has gone out in his soul and he agrees to join Schofield in settling up the score.

Schofield is eager to try his hand at killing. Taking justice into his own hands provides him with the excuse to aim his gun at another human being and pull the trigger. And indeed he is the one who shoots and kills the cowboy. Yet upon doing so, he is immediately filled with an overwhelming sense of self-loathing and remorse and he turns for comfort to Munny, a man who knows well that the business of settling scores is a deeply troubling one. As Schofield tries to reassure himself that the cowboy deserved his fate, Munny turns to him and says, "We all have it coming, kid."

While there was a sort of justice meted out in this film, it was parlayed by men who lived unjust lives themselves. In effect, they were in no position to stand in judgment over anyone else, because in the end, they deserved the same fate as their victims. This is not true of God, however. It is appropriate for God to stand in judgment over us, for he is absolutely just. God's hands are not stained. Moreover, God abhors injustice; there is no condoning it in God's universe. God is a God of order. God created out of the chaos a world where injustice and disorder have no place. So he is left with a deeply troubling problem. God cannot simply turn his back on our sin. To excuse even one offense reintroduces primordial chaos into the universe.

We know this well. We have laws that address even the smallest violations. And we are well aware of the consequences of letting unjust behavior go unpunished. There is a cheapness to forgiveness without justice that we as a society cannot afford to tolerate. This is also true for God. Justice cannot be set aside in order to let us off the hook. There must be a reckoning for our behavior, for we all sin to some degree or another. So in the end, as Munny says, we all have it coming to us. What hope is there for us?

FOR DISCUSSION

1. If we conclude that none of us is able ultimately to thwart the manifestation of sin in our lives, was it absolutely necessary that Jesus make atonement on our behalf?

2. Why couldn't God simply look the other way?

3. Can you think of people or characters who believe they are more worthy before God than another? Why is this sinful? What is the result?

4. What can be gained from recognizing that because we are human nothing we do can ever be perfect? Why not just quit trying?

GOD'S DEATH IS OUR SALVATION

So God was left with the choice of either losing his entire creation forever or assuming himself the consequences of our thoughtless sins. We see throughout the Bible how God is always reaching out to a humanity that consistently turns its back on him. In the end, having exhausted all other options, God was left with only one more—assuming himself the consequences of our thoughtless sins. And, it cost God his life. In his letter to the Romans Paul proclaims this extraordinary decision: "God proves his love for us in that while we still were sinners Christ died for us" (Rom 5:8). The God who upholds justice serves out the sentence we so justly deserve. This is what the cross is all about.

On Good Friday, a just God bears his own wrath against sin. In fact, God became a human being for the express purpose of accepting the sentence handed down upon us. On the cross, Jesus Christ who knew no sin, who was blameless in every way, took our sin upon himself. In a moment of monumental suffering, unknown to humanity before, the weight and punishment of all our sins, past and future, from the beginning of time to its end, were laid on him. There will never be a moment in human history more excruciating. We hear this in Jesus' anguished words, "My God, my God, why have you forsaken me?" (Mk 15:34). Jesus becomes forsaken, "unforgiven," for all of us.

In ancient Israel on the Day of Atonement, the priest would choose a lamb and symbolically place on it the sins of the members of the community. This lamb became the scapegoat, vested with the sin of Israel. It would be released into the wilderness, forever an outcast, sent to die in the desert. On the cross Jesus, the Lamb of God, became just such an outcast, our scapegoat. On him was placed all our iniquities. In a split-second he drew into himself the sum total of our disobedience. Jesus' sacrifice demonstrates at one and the same time God's justice and God's mercy. God hates sin too much to let it rend his universe. God loves us too much to let us be damned. So God becomes vested with our sins, despised and rejected himself.

FOR DISCUSSION

1. Can you think of instances in the Bible where God reached out only to have humanity turn its back on him?
2. What do you think of God's plan to rescue us?
3. How had you understood Jesus' death before?
4. Has that changed now?

SUMMARY

The good news is that not only does Jesus make everlasting atonement for our sins on the cross, his death and resurrection create the possibility for us to begin to live life differently, now. While it is true that our misdeeds are forgiven, it is also true that the power sin has over our lives is now broken. How can this be? On the cross Jesus bore all our sins and died under the weight of them. Yet on the third day after his death and burial he was raised from the dead. His glorious and remarkable resurrection means that the condition we all suffer from, the propensity to sin, need no longer rule our lives. Jesus' death and subsequent resurrection broke the determining power of the forces of sin over human existence. It is now possible for our nature to be re-aligned.

SESSION THREE

THE BAPTISMAL VOWS

In the service of Holy Baptism, we are invited to "turn to Jesus Christ and accept him as our savior" (Appendix, 101). The first step in this process is to admit, like a recovering addict, that we are powerless over sin. In effect, "sin" is our addiction and we must acknowledge it. When we recognize our compulsion and that we cannot break this "habit" ourselves, we are in agreement with St. Augustine when he declared we are unable not to sin. Unless we can come to this realization, we will unwittingly be held captive for the rest of our lives to our selfish motivations and desires.

Furthermore, we are called to acknowledge that there are forces and structures in our society and the world, bent on waging destruction and promoting enmity, which harness this capacity we all have for sin. By responding, "I renounce them," to the following questions: "Do you renounce Satan and all the spiritual forces of wickedness that rebel against God? Do you renounce the evil powers of this world which corrupt and destroy the creatures of God? Do you renounce all sinful desires that draw you from the love of God?" we publicly recognize our addiction and our intention to resist all evil forces that seek to entice us to participate in corporate manifestations of sin such as racism, genocide, and poverty.

The second step is to place our faith in Jesus Christ, who is triumphant over individual and communal sin. He alone, through the power of his resurrection, can bring forth in us what we can never completely do ourselves. He can dull our impulse to be self-centered and whet our appetite for selfless living. By turning to Jesus Christ and accepting him as our savior, the potential for holiness God created in all human beings can now unfold more fully in our life. He can redirect our wills so that, under his guidance, we become more and more gracious, generous, and more authentically humble, less preoccupied with our own needs and more eager to give sacrificially of ourselves.

Jesus is capable of changing the course our lives would take if we were left to our own devices. Through faith in him we can become a new creation. Yet our faith can only be placed in *Jesus* to accomplish this over the course of our lives, not in some misguided notion of our own ability. Every day we must recall our vow and acknowledge that he alone can save us.

Yet, intentionally or not, we will still on occasion fall short. We are not to fear, though, that our actions will lead God to abandon us. Having given up his life for us there is nothing we can do to cause him to turn away from us. God's love will never be denied us. However, many people have a difficult time accepting the fact that God loves them despite their failings and misdeeds. We discover, painfully, that our fellow human beings do withhold their love when we hurt them. But this is not true of God.

In his gospel, the evangelist Luke records a story Jesus tells his followers to illustrate this truth (Lk 15:11–24). The younger son of a man who owned property demanded one day that his father give him his inheritance on the spot. Not only was this quite peculiar—only at death was one's estate divided—it also put the father at a great disadvantage, for it gave him much less to live on while he remained alive. The younger son was getting, in effect, much more than he would have gotten upon his father's death. His callousness is obvious.

This son then proceeds to go abroad and spend his money recklessly. Soon, penniless and friendless, desperate for food and shelter, he turns to feeding pigs for a local farmer. It is among the swine that he comes to his senses. He resolves to return home and ask his father's forgiveness. He does not expect to be received back as a son, but rather as a hired hand, for even this is more than he deserves. He is well aware how deeply he has hurt his father.

Yet in telling this story, Jesus makes a point of noting that, from a distance, the father catches a glimpse of his returning son.

He is leading us to conclude that the father has been searching the horizon in the hope that his son would come back. This is not a man who intends to punish a selfish and ungrateful son. This is a father who desperately wants his wayward child back. He is resolved to receive his son into the household again, even before the son can blurt out his apology. The father never stopped loving his son and was willing and eager to do anything to get him back.

This story teaches us that God loves each of us unconditionally. We place our faith in a loving God, a God who gives up his life for us while knowing we will still hurt him. We never run out of second chances with God. It is essential we grasp this truth, so that we do not despair in our inability to refrain from falling short. The worst thing that could happen would be for us to lose hope in God's love for us, for it is precisely the love of God that is able to transform our unruly nature. In the service of Holy Baptism we are given the opportunity to embrace this good news and place our "whole trust in God's grace and love" (Appendix, 101).

Paul emphasized this truth when he wrote, "If God is for us, who is against us? He who did not withhold his own Son, but gave him up for all of us, will he not with him also give us everything else? ...For I am convinced that neither death, nor life, nor angels, nor rulers, nor things present, nor things to come, nor powers, nor height, nor depth, nor anything else in all creation will be able to separate us from the love of God in Christ Jesus our Lord" (Rom 8:31b–32, 38–39).

Finally, the gulf between us and the love God has for humanity that arose as a result of our wayward natures—captured so well in the story of Adam and Eve—is now closed forever through the death and resurrection of Jesus Christ. Despite our sins we should never doubt God's love for us. God can do marvelous things in our life when we place our trust in him.

FOR DISCUSSION

1. Have you ever felt you were loved unconditionally?
2. Why might we feel unworthy of such love when we fall short?
3. Does it make a difference to you to know that nothing you can do can separate you from the love of God?

Having accepted Jesus as our Savior and placed our trust in his grace and love we are now ready to commit to being his disciples. The final question asked of baptismal candidates has to do with discipleship: "Do you promise to follow and obey him as your Lord?" (Appendix, 101). We are saved from the debilitating power of sin so that we can focus our attention beyond ourselves and go forth and carry on God's work in the world. It would be helpful at this point to review some of the points from Chapter 2 concerning discipleship.

As we saw in the description of a third-century baptismal service (54–55), baptism is a metaphorical death. The vows we have just looked at are very clear in renouncing anything that gets in the way of our commitment to Jesus.

BEING A DISCIPLE

Let's turn to the last several questions asked in the Baptismal Covenant (Appendix, 103).

"Will you continue in the apostles' teaching and fellowship, in the breaking of bread, and in the prayers?

"Will you persevere in resisting evil, and, whenever you fall into sin, repent and return to the Lord?

"Will you proclaim by word and example the Good News of God in Christ?

"Will you seek and serve Christ in all persons, loving your neighbor as yourself?

"Will you strive for justice and peace among all people, and respect the dignity of every human being?"

The response to each one is "I will, with God's help."

Each of these questions leads us to an understanding what being a disciple is all about. As we have seen throughout this discussion, a disciple is one who:

- attends worship regularly, to honor and praise God;
- is committed to learning more about the faith;
- understands the importance of being in fellowship with other people of faith for mutual support and encouragement;
- develops a habit of regular prayer, in order to seek God's will in his life and to intercede on behalf of the needs of others.

Furthermore, a disciple is someone who is aware of her own propensity to sin and does not overestimate her ability to resist temptation. When she does fall short, she is not afraid to admit it to herself and to God. In fact, she makes a point of reviewing her day in prayer with God before retiring for the night. She seeks God's forgiveness for her wrongdoings and places her trust anew in God's love and grace.

A disciple recognizes that on any day he has the opportunity to witness to the Good News of God in Jesus Christ. It may simply be in the way he conducts his life—with patience, kindness, humility and generosity—that he gives such witness. He disciplines himself to be Christ-like in all situations, since others can be led to seek Christ simply as a result of his example. He is ready to give an account of his faith should someone make inquiry.

A disciple seeks Christ in all persons, not just in those whom she likes or admires, or whom she expects to treat her well. She diligently reminds herself to seek Christ in those who are rude or selfish or mean-spirited, since Jesus gave up his life for them also. She recognizes that the term "neighbor" applies to everyone whom God has created and tries to love them as she loves herself.

In striving for justice and peace, a disciple is cognizant of the fact that he could be putting his life in danger, for others will be threatened by such efforts. It means he is committed to working to change a system that keeps poor people poor and encourages inequity and discrimination. He keeps in mind that his is the kingdom of God, for blessed are those who are persecuted for righteousness' sake (Mt 5:10).

FOR DISCUSSION

1. Discuss the questions from the Baptismal Covenant that are listed above (76). What do you think they are calling you to do?

2. How consistent are you in these areas? Perhaps participants who have found ways to be more consistent can share their experience with the other members of the group.

3. Do you have further suggestions as to what it means to be a disciple?

4. Read the following passage: "Then Jesus said to them all, 'If any want to become my followers, let them deny themselves and take up their cross daily and follow me. For those who want to save their life will lose it, and those who lose their life for my sake will save it'" (Lk 9:23–25). How does this speak to you?

5. Re-read the quote from Dietrich Bonhoeffer (24). What can compromise our allegiance to Jesus these days?

CHAPTER 6

PRIVILEGES AND RESPONSIBILITIES OF BELONGING

In preparing for baptism, it is important to spend time coming to terms with the consequences that arise from one's official entry into the Christian community. Baptism, as an initiation, carries with it certain privileges and responsibilities that the candidate—or the candidate's family—should be prepared to accept. Yet our modern understanding of what it means to belong to something is often skewed because we tend to value the wants and rights of an individual over the needs of the community. This final session is designed to help you discover what belonging to the Christian community is all about.

THE FINAL SESSION

Christians often confuse membership in their particular Christian community with membership in secular communities. They see their involvement as voluntary, assuming they are entering a community geared toward meeting their individual needs. When they give of their resources, they expect something in return.

FOR DISCUSSION

Let's begin this discussion by making another list. The moderator should record these answers on a sheet of newsprint.

1. Take out your wallets and look at your membership cards.
2. What organizations or communities you belong to?
3. What makes each of these groups to which you belong a community?
4. What binds the members together?
5. How is the group governed?
6. What is the nature of your commitment to it?
7. What might cause you to terminate your commitment?

Most of us belong to secular communities because they offer us a particular advantage. It is in our best interest to join. We are offered choices and options that serve to benefit us in some way. In this sense belonging is about optimizing our pursuits and concerns. Accordingly, we belong for self-interested reasons and we tend to feel no qualms about walking away when we perceive belonging is no longer to our advantage. It is simply a matter of economics that everyone takes for granted.

On the other hand, belonging to the Christian community is radically different from belonging to other organizations or groups. Ultimately we did not make the choice to belong; instead it is God's choice to draw us to him through his son, Jesus Christ. God has led us to the parish in which we are members. Of course we gave our consent, but we must remember that it is God who took the initiative. And in giving our consent we are moving from a realm where we act out of a concern for our individual rights and wants and into the realm of Christian community where we focus instead upon the common good. We are not the center of attention. Our own particular interests do not determine the direction of the group. Our membership is not to be understood as voluntary. We do not state the terms under which we will join.

Belonging in this way makes claims upon our lives that we cannot walk away from even when we feel we are being inconvenienced. As the writer of the letter to the Ephesians states, "we are members of one another" (Eph 4:25b).

Unfortunately, today many Christians equate belonging to the Christian community with belonging to a secular organization. We are accustomed to thinking first about our own needs and wants. We see ourselves as individuals who have gathered voluntarily for our own particular interests. Choice is what holds us together. We exist as a community to the extent our individual interests overlap. Sadly, we often feel no overriding sense of obligation to others in the group.

FOR DISCUSSION

1. What happens when we apply our criteria for membership in a secular community to our sense of belonging to a Christian community?

2. How would this affect the dynamics of your parish?

3. Can you think of ways you experienced God's call to this class, to this parish, or to this denomination?

THE HOLY SPIRIT

What makes membership in the Christian community so different? In order to fully understand, it is helpful to review the role of the Holy Spirit in baptism as presented in the following account of the coming of the Holy Spirit in the Acts of the Apostles:

> When the day of Pentecost had come, they were all together in one place. And suddenly from heaven there came a sound like the rush of a violent wind, and it filled the entire house where they were sitting. Divided tongues, as of fire, appeared among them, and a tongue rested on each of them.

> All of them were filled with the Holy Spirit and began to speak in other languages, as the Spirit gave them ability. Now there were devout Jews from every nation under heaven living in Jerusalem. And at this sound the crowd gathered and was bewildered, because each one heard them speaking in the native language of each. Amazed and astonished, they asked, "Are not all these who are speaking Galileans? And how is it that we hear, each of us, in our own native language? Parthians, Medes, Elamites, and residents of Mesopotamia, Judea and Cappadocia, Pontus and Asia, Phrygia and Pamphylia, Egypt and the parts of Libya belonging to Cyrene, and visitors from Rome, both Jews and proselytes, Cretans and Arabs—in our own languages we hear them speaking about God's deeds of power. All were amazed and perplexed, saying to one another, "What does this mean?" (Acts 2:1–12)

Recall the very different experience of the people in the story of the tower of Babel in Genesis (10–11). But now, at Pentecost, through the power of the Holy Spirit, people who cannot converse with one another because of the barrier of language are suddenly able, despite that hindrance, to communicate about what is most important to human existence: the saving death and resurrection of Jesus Christ. It is now possible for human beings to thrive in community despite the usual obstacles that arise as a result of sin. In fact, community is now central to the lives of those who follow Jesus. It is to be the realm in which they experience the presence of God.

Moreover, the Holy Spirit gives power to those who are Jesus' witnesses. The apostles, undereducated at best and inexperienced at preaching and teaching, are now able, through the Holy Spirit, to proclaim boldly the essentials of the gospel.

> Now when they [the crowds] heard this [Peter's spontaneous sermon], they were cut to the heart and said to Peter and to the other apostles, "Brothers, what should we do?" Peter said to them, "Repent, and be baptized every one of you in the name of Jesus Christ so that your sins may be forgiven; and you will receive the gift of the Holy Spirit. For the promise is for you, for your children, and for all who are far away,

everyone whom the Lord our God calls to him." And he testified with many other arguments and exhorted them, saying, "Save yourselves from this corrupt generation." So those who welcomed his message were baptized, and that day about three thousand persons were added. They devoted themselves to the apostles' teaching and fellowship, to the breaking of bread and the prayers. Awe came upon everyone, because many wonders and signs were being done by the apostles. All who believed were together and had all things in common; they would sell their possessions and goods and distribute the proceeds to all, as any had need. Day by day, as they spent much time together in the temple, they broke bread at home and ate their food with glad and generous hearts, praising God and having the goodwill of all the people. And day by day the Lord added to their number those who were being saved. (Acts 2:37-47)

This account shows a link between baptism and the work of the Holy Spirit. The apostles, under the power of the Holy Spirit, are able to present the news of the life, death, and resurrection of Jesus Christ in such a way that other people, complete strangers, are captivated. In response to this preaching they ask to be baptized, whereupon they too are filled with the Holy Spirit and band together in communities. These communities are characterized by a high degree of mutual love and support. In fact, everyone who is baptized and receives the Holy Spirit is bound up in a community; no one remains outside of one.

We further hear in Paul's first letter to the Corinthians how the Holy Spirit apportions gifts and talents to each member so that they are empowered to carry on ministry for the good of the entire community: "To each is given the manifestation of the Spirit for the common good" (1 Cor 12:7).

ALL MEMBERS ARE MINSTERS

Therefore, everyone who is baptized is empowered by the Holy Spirit to carry on various ministries for the good of—and on behalf of—the congregation. *All baptized members are ministers.*

As members of the Christian community we need to accept our mutual dependence upon one another, even though this may seem unnatural or uncomfortable in our modern society. Furthermore, we are to value and utilize one another's contributions. Once again, Paul underscores this point:

> Indeed, the body does not consist of one member but of many. If the foot would say, "Because I am not a hand, I do not belong to the body," that would not make it any less a part of the body. And if the ear would say, "Because I am not an eye, I do not belong to the body," that would not make it any less a part of the body. If the whole body were an eye, where would the hearing be: If the whole body were hearing, where would the sense of smell be? But as it is, God arranged the members in the body, each one of them, as he chose. If all were a single member, where would the body be? As it is, there are many members, yet one body. The eye cannot say to the hand, "I have no need of you," nor again the head to the feet, "I have no need of you." On the contrary, the members of the body that seem to be weaker are indispensable, and those members of the body that we think less honorable we clothe with greater honor, and our less respectable members are treated with greater respect; whereas our more respectable members do not deed this. But God has so arranged the body, giving greater honor to the inferior member, that there may be no dissension within the body, but the members may have the same care for one another. If one member suffers, all suffer together with it; if one member is honored, all rejoice together with it. Now you are the body of Christ and individually members of it. (1 Cor 12:14–27)

In this passage, Paul was addressing members of the congregation he founded in Corinth. He had been informed, while away on a missionary journey, that conflict had arisen among those whom belonged to the various house churches. It seems that members were arguing with one another over who possessed spiritual gifts of greater importance. We also know from Paul's correspondence with the church in Corinth that wealthier members were snubbing the poorer ones and excluding them from some of the fellowship activities, and that several members were suing one another in civil court. What we see displayed here is an unhealthy tendency to focus upon the needs and wants of the individual or a small group of elitists rather than upon the good of the community as a whole.

Paul is shocked at the news of their behavior toward one another. He uses the analogy of a human body to make the point that every member is important to the community. The community cannot afford to lose, exclude, or devalue any one. Everyone has been given gifts to contribute to the common good and every gift is essential. There is no hierarchy of talent. In fact, members who are of less means should be given greater honor. And all members must learn to work together with mutual respect and care and never lose sight of the precept that the needs of the community come before the wants of individuals within it.

Through the gift of the Holy Spirit in baptism, we have all been given talent that needs to be shared with the community for its proper functioning and well being. Everyone plays an important role in building up the church. The ministers of the church are not just those who are ordained. Every lay person is a minister, also. Since "Holy Baptism is full initiation by water and the Holy Spirit into Christ's Body the Church" (Appendix, 95), even children and babies are empowered for ministry. Therefore it is essential that we raise them with the understanding that they have something to offer the congregation—as well as the understanding that the congregation has something to offer them. It is a relationship of mutuality.

FOR DISCUSSION

1. What gifts are necessary within your church for the good of the community?

2. Have you ever thought of yourselves as ministers in this way before?

3. What does Paul's passage about gifts say to you?

CHILDREN ARE MINISTERS TOO

There are a number of simple ways for parents to impart a sense of ministry to their children. The following are suggested ways to help children grow up with an appreciation for their role as ministers within the congregation:

1. *Set time aside for the entire family to carry on a ministry to the congregation outside of worship.* Perhaps in your parish, at Christmas and Easter, flowers used to adorn the church are taken afterwards to the homes of members who are shut-in. This is a simple and meaningful ministry for families to undertake. Also, the church may have a Saturday set aside for the congregation to participate in yard work or repairs. Even small children can pull weeds. What is important is that they feel as though they are contributing to the good of the church and its members.

2. *Offer your child the opportunity to serve as a liturgical assistant in worship.* Many churches have a children's and youth choir. As children grow older they may also participate as acolytes and lectors. Some parishes also license young persons who have reached the age of sixteen to serve as a chalice bearer. It is very satisfying for children to grow up feeling that they have something to contribute to the congregation's services of worship.

3. *Encourage your child to share, on behalf of the congregation, time and talent in ministries within the larger community where you reside.* Many towns and cities have at least one soup kitchen for people who are hungry and possibly homeless. These community services are always in need of servers. This is another ministry in which the family could possibly participate together. There may be an opportunity for your child to tutor children at a local school. Some churches adopt a highway in town for periodic cleaning. Furthermore, the local Girl or Boy Scouts honors a child's religious beliefs while encouraging public service to the larger community.

4. *Set an example of pledging financial resources to the congregation. Encourage your child to make a pledge.* It is important for all baptized people to give of their time, talent, *and* treasure. One's pledge benefits the entire community, including oneself. It is essential that all members see it as their responsibility to support ministries, programs, and general church upkeep financially as well as practically. Everyone must give of their resources for the common good.

Volunteer or Minster?

Being a volunteer and being a minister are two very different things. Volunteerism has a long a noble history in our country. Yet anyone who has worked in the non-profit sector knows the downside to volunteerism: what is freely offered can also be suddenly withdrawn, without notice. Organizations are often left scrambling to cover duties assigned to a volunteer who, because of a change in plans or a decreased level of interest, has not shown up. Depending solely on the hope that an individual is feeling kind-hearted enough to report for work is not always an efficient business practice. In truth, the level of commitment can vary greatly from volunteer to volunteer. Some are incredibly dedicated and consistently dependable; others are not.

In many churches there is a tendency to think of the people who give freely of their time and treasure to the support of the congregation as "volunteers," but this is not a particularly helpful label. It is a purely secular term implying that one's level of commitment is a private matter that can wax and wane at whim. Such a notion is certainly at odds with a biblical understanding of commitment. Christians are not volunteers, but ministers.

One ministers, not because one is feeling generous on a particular day, but rather out of a sense of faithfulness—indeed, obedience—to God. Ministry is not withdrawn when it is no longer convenient. In fact, ministry is often inconvenient, for there is always an element of sacrifice to it. God calls us to present ourselves—our time, talent and treasure, as "a living sacrifice, holy and accept-able to God" (Rom 12:1).

For Discussion

1. What is the difference between being a volunteer and being a minister?
2. In what ways do you see yourself exercising a ministry either for your church or on behalf of your church?
3. In what other ways can your children share their gifts and talents with the congregation?

Baptism, as well as One's Faith, Is not a Private Matter

To end where we began, it is vital to remember that *Christianity is personal, but not private*. It is consummately social. Our faith is to be lived out within the context of the community of fellow Christians to which we belong. This is made clear from the moment of our baptism. Baptism does not take place in private. It is not a matter of concern for only the minister, the candidate, and the family. The Book of Common Prayer makes clear that all baptisms should take place "within the Eucharist as the chief service on a Sunday or other feast." (Appendix, 95) The congregation plays an essential role in every baptism, because the sacrament of baptism belongs to the entire church.

At the beginning of the service, after the candidates and their sponsors make their vows, the congregation makes one also. The celebrant addresses the congregation saying, "Will you who witness these vows do all in your power to support these persons in their life in Christ?" The congregation responds, "We will" (Appendix, 101).

Furthermore, after the baptism itself, the celebrant and congregation both proclaim, "We receive you into the household of God. Confess the faith of Christ crucified, proclaim his resurrection, and share with us in his eternal priesthood" (Appendix, 107). In effect, the congregation has the last word before the Peace is exchanged.

As the session comes to a close, discuss the usefulness of these preparatory sessions. Do you view baptism any differently now? If so, how?

CONCLUSION OF THE FINAL SESSION

If so desired, the final session may end with a rehearsal for the Service of Baptism and conclude with the following collect.

For All Baptized Christians

Grant, Lord God, to all who have been baptized into the death and resurrection of your Son Jesus Christ, that, as we have put away the old life of sin, so we may be renewed in the spirit of our minds, and live in righteousness and true holiness; through Jesus Christ our Lord, who lives and reigns with you, in the unity of the Holy Spirit, one God, now and for ever. *Amen.**

---

* BCP, 252.

CHAPTER 7

BUILDING A STRONGER CHURCH

A NOTE FOR ORDAINED MINISTERS AND MEMBERS OF THEIR CONGREGATIONS

In the early centuries of Christianity no one would have assumed that a person was ready for baptism simply because he or she expressed an interest in being baptized. Undertaking such a radical way of life required that time be set aside for self-evaluation, for moral instruction and eventually, for theological training. And, in the previous chapters, we have come to recognize that modern candidates for baptism, or their parents, come as unformed as did those in the early life of the church.

Therefore, candidates also need to spend time in preparation today. They too need to learn about the two central elements of baptism—belonging and discipleship—because so many of the messages in our culture run counter to them. Additionally, since civil religion is actually more a function of social mores than an authentic Christian way of life, candidates need to understand the difference between the two. The cost in not doing so is too great.

When a congregation and its ordained ministers embrace the responsibility to prepare people for baptism—in addition to offering ongoing programs of study to explore the implications of baptismal vows for those already baptized—not only is the parish providing formation in the basics of Christian living and believing, they are building a stronger church. Congregations need committed and informed lay people, people who are serious about the call to ministry within and beyond the parish, people who may also be eager to help prepare others who have come for baptism, reaffirmation, or renewal of baptismal vows.

But in order for this to happen fully, the clergy person must be committed to taking the time to develop such programs. All too often , however, parish clergy are inundated with many other demands upon their time. Pastoral issues, committee concerns, and administrative needs all vie for the clergy person's attention. Yet, it is also true that clergy get bogged down in things that, from a practical and spiritual point of view, are better left in the capable hands of the laity.

The ministry of parish clergy is largely to empower and equip the laity to carry on ministry. This can be accomplished in a variety of ways, chiefly through preaching, teaching, administering the sacraments, careful preparation for services of worship, and spiritual counseling. A lay person who has been given a grounding in the faith and receives encouragement and support from their parish priest can rightfully undertake any number of duties that take clergy away from their principal obligations.

Lay people gifted with administrative skills can staff and run committee meetings. Others can assume some administrative tasks and office work. Once equipped, lay people can provide pastoral care and disciple other lay people. They can address issues of justice and righteousness in the larger community. In essence, the laity can take up the ministry that is rightfully theirs—when the clergy person is committed to spending his or her time preparing them to do just that. And it all begins with a thorough understanding of baptism and its privileges and responsibilities.

According to the Book of Common Prayer the ministry of lay persons is "To represent Christ and his Church; to bear witness to him wherever they may be; and, according to the gifts given them, to carry on Christ's work of reconciliation in the world; and to take their place in the life, worship, and governance of the Church."* However, over the years there has been some confusion regarding the respective roles of the ordained ministers and of the laity. For a very long time clergy were thought to be the only ones who performed ministry and the laity were the ones to whom the clergy ministered. This emphasis began to shift significantly in the late seventies as Christians everywhere began to recover their rightful call to ministry by virtue of their baptism.

Yet this rediscovery has not always been enthusiastically accepted. Members of congregations, long accustomed to the clergy being the only ministers, are sometimes reluctant to embrace their own ministry. And even when they do so, there are still some who feel that a meeting, a social occasion, or a lay-led pastoral or administrative ministry is not legitimate unless a clergy person is present. Sadly, there are those people who believe that no one will take a meeting or a ministry seriously unless a priest is leading it.

The clergy person who resolves to change this unfortunate point of view must be prepared to face a fair amount of resistance and ensuing conflict. At times, it may seem that it is just not worth the trouble. Yet working through such resistance, determined to empower and equip the laity to take up their ministry is, in essence, what clergy are instructed to do at their ordination. The bishop calls us "to work as a pastor, priest and teacher... and to nourish Christ's people from the riches of his grace, and strengthen them to glorify God in this life and in the life to come."+

In truth, there is also resistance on the part of clergy to give over what seemingly amounts to power to the laity. When clergy

---

* BCP, 855.

+ BCP, 531.

say that it is easier in the long run to do things themselves, no matter how harried they are, they may also have a hidden agenda.

Yet in fairness to my brother and sister clerics, I know how difficult it is to begin to do the kind of teaching and formation necessary to equip and empower lay persons. Although I received a fine seminary education, at no point in those three years of study was I taught how to teach the faith. I was taught the faith; but I was not taught how to teach it to others. It is one thing to have knowledge. It is another thing altogether to know how to pass it on in a clear and concise way.

It took me years to begin to figure out what the members of the congregations I served needed to know most and how to convey them: the essentials of theology, church history, the Bible, hermeneutics, liturgy, and a Christian perspective on moral and pastoral issues. Some courses were relatively easy for which to organize and prepare, such as a study of the Book of Common Prayer, Episcopal Church history and polity, and the practical aspects of living a Christian life. Others, such as a study of particular books of the Bible, issues involved in seeking to interpret the Bible, and the theological concerns that led to the formulation of the Nicene Creed were more difficult because I found gaps in my own understanding of these subjects.

It is time for clergy to reclaim their ministry of teaching, and time for seminaries to train their clergy how to carry out this ministry. The time and effort spent recovering this ministry, not only in preparing people for baptism, but in continuing formation after baptism, will be of great benefit to individual congregations and their members as well as to the church at large.

It is also true that clergy are not always the only people able to take up the ministry of teaching. In any given parish there may well be informed lay people who are so-equipped and they should be given every opportunity to share their gifts. Teaching is not the exclusive domain of the clergy. The more lay participation in all areas of ministry, particularly in the ministry of teaching, the better for all.

However, *every* ordained person has received a seminary education or an equivalent. Even if they have not been trained in how to teach the faith, they have at least studied it intensively for three years and understand the pitfalls that can arise in Bible study or in a parish theological course, when participants lack the perspective that comes from having studied the conflicts and heresies throughout church history and the subtle issues that have to do with interpreting Scripture. Not every lay person can offer this perspective, yet all clergy should be able to. Therefore, clergy also must see themselves as teachers and exercise the authority granted to them through ordination for equipping the Body of Christ.

Taking baptismal preparation—and Christian formation in general—seriously, through teaching, as well as preaching, liturgical preparation. and spiritual counseling may require a re-prioritizing of time and effort that may not be initially well received by everyone in the parish. However, doing so will help members of the congregation embrace the ministry given to them by the Holy Spirit at baptism and will lead to a deepening of commitment and faithfulness.

Consequently, taking baptism seriously can become an exciting revolution within the church for the good of all.

THE SERVICE OF HOLY BAPTISM ACCORDING TO THE BOOK OF COMMON PRAYER

CONCERNING THE SERVICE

Holy Baptism is full initiation by water and the Holy Spirit into Christ's Body the Church. The bond which God establishes in Baptism is indissoluble. **(Chapter 3, 39 and Chapter 6, 85)**

Holy Baptism is appropriately administered within the Eucharist as the chief service on a Sunday or other feast. **(Chapter 6, 88)**

The bishop, when present, is the celebrant; and is expected to preach the Word and preside at Baptism and the Eucharist. At Baptism, the bishop officiates at the Presentation and Examination of the Candidates; says the Thanksgiving over the Water; [consecrates the Chrism;] reads the prayer, "Heavenly Father, we thank you that by water and the Holy Spirit;" and officiates at what follows.

In the absence of a bishop, a priest is the celebrant and presides at the service. If a priest uses Chrism in signing the newly baptized, it must have been previously consecrated by the bishop.

Each candidate for Holy Baptism is to be sponsored by one or more baptized persons.

Sponsors of adults and older children present their candidates and thereby signify their endorsement of the candidates and their intention to support them by prayer and example in their Christian life. Sponsors of infants, commonly called godparents, present their candidates, make promises in their own names, and also take vows on behalf of their candidates.

It is fitting that parents be included among the godparents of their own children. Parents and godparents are to be instructed in the meaning of Baptism, in their duties to help the new Christians grow in the knowledge and love of God, and in their responsibilities as members of his Church. **(Chapters 4, 5 and 6)**

HOLY BAPTISM

A hymn, psalm, or anthem may be sung.

The people standing, the Celebrant says

	Blessed be God: Father, Son, and Holy Spirit.
People	And blessed be his kingdom, now and for ever. Amen.

In place of the above, from Easter Day through the Day of Pentecost

Celebrant	Alleluia. Christ is risen.
People	The Lord is risen indeed. Alleluia.

In Lent and on other penitential occasions

Celebrant	Bless the Lord who forgives all our sins.
People	His mercy endures for ever.

The Celebrant then continues

	There is one Body and one Spirit;
People	There is one hope in God's call to us;
Celebrant	One Lord, one Faith, one Baptism;
People	One God and Father of all.

Celebrant	The Lord be with you.
People	And also with you.
Celebrant	Let us pray.

THE COLLECT OF THE DAY

People   Amen.

At the principal service on a Sunday or other feast, the Collect and Lessons are properly those of the Day. On other occasions they are selected from "At Baptism."

THE LESSONS

The people sit. Once or two Lessons, as appointed, are read, the Reader first saying

A Reading (Lesson) from _____.

A citation giving chapter and verse may be added.

After each Reading, the Reader may say

   The Word of the Lord.
People   Thanks be to God.

Or the Reader may say   Here ends the Reading (Epistle).

Silence may follow.

A Psalm, hymn, or anthem may follow each Reading.

Then, all standing, the Deacon or a Priest reads the Gospel, first saying

   The Holy Gospel of our Lord Jesus Christ
   According to _____.

People   Glory to you, Lord Christ.

After the Gospel, the Reader says

The Gospel of the Lord.

People   Praise to you, Lord, Christ.

The Sermon

Or the Sermon may be preached after the Peace.

PRESENTATION AND EXAMINATION
OF THE CANDIDATES

The Celebrant says

The Candidate(s) for Holy Baptism will now be presented.

ADULTS AND OLDER CHILDREN

The candidates who are able to answer for themselves are presented individually by their Sponsors, as follows

Sponsor   I present N. to receive the Sacrament of Baptism.

The Celebrant asks each candidate when presented

Do you desire to be baptized?

Candidate   I do.

INFANTS AND YOUNGER CHILDREN

Then the candidates unable to answer for themselves are presented individually by their Parents and Godparents, as follows

Parents and Godparents

I present N. to receive the Sacrament of Baptism.

When all have been presented the Celebrant asks the parents and godparents

Will you be responsible for seeing that the child you present is brought up in the Christian faith and life? **(See Chapter 4, 60)**

Parents and Godparents

I will, with God's help.

Celebrant

Will you by your prayers and witness help this child to grow into the full stature of Christ? **(See Chapter 4, 59)**

Parents and Godparents
I will, with God's help.

Then the Celebrant asks the following questions of the candidates who can speak for themselves, and of the parents and godparents who speak on behalf of the infants and younger children.

Question	Do you renounce Satan and all the spiritual forces of wickedness that rebel against God? **(Chapter 5, 66)**
Answer	I renounce them.
Question	Do you renounce the evil powers of this world which corrupt and destroy the creatures of God? **(Chapter 5, 66)**
Answer	I renounce them.
Question	Do you renounce all sinful desires that draw you from the love of God? **(Chapter 5, 66)**
Answer	I renounce them.
Question	Do you turn to Jesus Christ and accept him as your Savior? **(Chapter 5, 73)**
Answer	I do.
Question	Do you put your whole trust in his grace and love? **(Chapter 5, 75)**
Answer	I do.
Question	Do you promise to follow and obey him as your Lord?**(Chapter 2, 23; Chapter 5, 76)**
Answer	I do.

After all have been presented, the Celebrant addresses the congregation, saying

Will you who witness these vows do all in your power to support *these persons* in *their* life in Christ? **(Chapter 3, 45 and Chapter 6, 88)**

People	We will.

The Celebrant then says these or similar words

Let us join with *those* who *are* committing *themselves* to Christ and renew our own baptismal covenant.

THE BAPTISMAL COVENANT

Celebrant	Do you believe in God the Father?
People	I believe in God, the Father almighty,
	creator of heaven and earth.

Celebrant	Do you believe in Jesus Christ, the Son of God?
People	I believe in Jesus Christ, his only Son, our Lord.

He was conceived by the power of the
Holy Spirit
and born of the Virgin Mary.
He suffered under Pontius Pilate,
was crucified, died, and was buried.
He descended to the dead.
On the third day he rose again.
He ascended into heaven,
and is seated at the right hand of the Father.
He will come again to judge the living and the dead.

Celebrant	Do you believe in God the Holy Spirit?
People	I believe in the Holy Spirit,

the holy catholic Church,
the communion of saints,
the forgiveness of sins,
the resurrection of the body,
and the life everlasting.

Celebrant	Will you continue in the apostles' teaching and fellowship, in the breaking of bread, and in the prayers? **(Chapter 2, 31; Chapter 4, 59; Chapter 5, 76)**
People	I will, with God's help.
Celebrant	Will you persevere in resisting evil, and, whenever you fall into sin, repent and return to the Lord? **(Chapter 5, 76)**
People	I will, with God's help.
Celebrant	Will you proclaim by word and example the Good News of God in Christ? **(Chapter 2, 23; Chapter 5, 76)**
People	I will, with God's help.
Celebrant	Will you seek and serve Christ in all persons, loving your neighbor as yourself? **(Chapter 2, 23; Chapter 5, 76)**
People	I will, with God's help.
Celebrant	Will you strive for justice and peace among all people, and respect the dignity of every human being? **(Chapter 2, 23; Chapter 5, 76)**
People	I will, with God's help.

PRAYERS FOR THE CANDIDATES

The Celebrant then says to the congregation

Let us now pray for *these persons* who *are* to receive the Sacrament of new birth [and for those (this person) who *have* renewed *their* commitment to Christ.]

A Person appointed leads the following petitions

Leader　　　　Deliver *them*, O Lord, from the way of sin and death.

People　　　　Lord, hear our prayer.

Leader　　　　Open *their hearts* to your grace and truth.

People　　　　Lord, hear our prayer.

Leader　　　　Fill *them* with your holy and life-giving Spirit.

People　　　　Lord, hear our prayer.

Leader　　　　Keep *them* in the faith and communion of your holy Church.

People　　　　Lord, hear our prayer.

Leader　　　　Teach *them* to love others in the power of the Spirit.

People　　　　Lord, hear our prayer.

Leader　　　　Send *them* into the world in witness to your love.

People　　　　Lord, hear our prayer.

Leader　　　　Bring *them* to the fullness of your peace and glory.

People　　　　Lord, hear our prayer.

The Celebrant says

Grant, O Lord, that all who are baptized into the death
of Jesus Christ your Son may live in the power of his
resurrection and look for him to come again in glory; who
lives and reigns now and for ever. *Amen.* **(Chapter 2, 30)**

THANKSGIVING OVER THE WATER

The Celebrant blesses the water, first saying

	The Lord be with you.
People	And also with you.

Celebrant	Let us give thanks to the Lord our God.
People	It is right to give him thanks and praise.

Celebrant

We thank you, Almighty God, for the gift of water.
Over it the Holy Spirit moved in the beginning of creation.
Through it you led the children of Israel out of their bondage
in Egypt into the land of promise. In it your Son Jesus
received the baptism of John and was anointed by the Holy
Spirit as the Messiah, the Christ, to lead us, through his death
and resurrection, from the bondage of sin into everlasting life.
(Chapter 5)

We thank you, Father, for the water of Baptism. In it we are
buried with Christ in his death. By it we share in his
resurrection. **(Chapter 5)**
Through it we are reborn by the Holy Spirit.
Therefore in joyful obedience to your Son, we bring into his
fellowship those who come to him in faith, baptizing them in
the Name of the Father, and of the Son, and of the Holy Spirit.

At the following words, the Celebrant touches the water

Now sanctify this water, we pray you, by the power of your
Holy Spirit, that those who here are cleansed from sin and
born again may continue for ever in the risen life of Jesus
Christ our Savior.

To him, to you, and to the Holy Spirit, be all honor and glory, now and for ever. *Amen.*

CONSECRATION OF THE CHRISM

The Bishop may then consecrate oil of Chrism, placing a hand on the vessel of oil, and saying

Eternal Father, whose blessed Son was anointed by the Holy Spirit to be the Savior and servant of all, we pray you to consecrate this oil, that those who are sealed with it may share in the royal priesthood of Jesus Christ; who lives and reigns with you and the Holy Spirit, for ever and ever. *Amen.*

THE BAPTISM

Each candidate is presented by name to the Celebrant, or to an assisting priest or deacon, who then immerses, or pours water upon, the candidate, saying

N., I baptize you in the Name of the Father, and of the Son, and of the Holy Spirit. *Amen.*

When this action has been completed for all candidates, the Bishop or Priest, at a place in full sight of the congregation, prays over them, saying

Let us pray.

Heavenly Father, we thank you that by water and the Holy Spirit you have bestowed upon *these* your *servants* the forgiveness of sin, and have raised *them* to the new life of grace. Sustain *them*, O Lord, in your Holy Spirit. Give *them* an inquiring and discerning heart, the courage to will and to persevere, a spirit to know and to love you, and the gift of joy and wonder in all your works. *Amen.*

Then the Bishop or Priest places a hand on the person's head, marking on the forehead the sign of the cross [using Chrism if desired] and saying to each one

N., you are sealed by the Holy Spirit in Baptism and marked as Christ's own for ever. *Amen.*

Or this action may be done immediately after the administration of the water and before the preceding prayer.

When all have been baptized, the Celebrant says

Let us welcome the newly baptized.

Celebrant and People
We receive you into the household of God. Confess the faith of Christ crucified, proclaim his resurrection, and share with us in his eternal priesthood. **(Chapter 3, 40; Chapter 6, 89)**

If Confirmation, Reception, or the Reaffirmation of Baptismal Vows is not to follow, the Peace is now exchanged

Celebrant   The peace of the Lord be always with you.
People   And also with you.